Healthy Models for Relationships

The Basic Principles Behind Good Relationships With Your Partner, Family, Parents, Children, Friends, Colleagues and All the Other People in Your Life

Other books by Barbara Berger

The Road to Power – Fast Food for the Soul (Book 1 & 2)

Find and Follow Your Inner Compass – Instant Guidance in an Age of Information Overload

Sane Self Talk – Cultivating the Voice of Sanity Within

The Awakening Human Being – A Guide to the Power of Mind (with Tim Ray)

Are You Happy Now? 10 Ways to Live a Happy Life

The Spiritual Pathway – A Guide to the Joys of Awakening and Soul Evolution

Mental Technology – Software for Your Hardware

Gateway to Grace – Barbara Berger's Guide to User-Friendly Meditation

The Mental Laws – Understanding the Way the Mind Works

The Adventures of Pebble Beach (a novel)

Healthy Models for Relationships

The Basic Principles Behind Good
Relationships With Your Partner, Family,
Parents, Children, Friends, Colleagues
and All the Other People in Your Life

Barbara Berger

Edited by Tim Ray

BOOKS

Winchester, UK
Washington, USA

JOHN HUNT PUBLISHING

First published by O-Books, 2023
O-Books is an imprint of John Hunt Publishing Ltd., 3 East St., Alresford,
Hampshire SO24 9EE, UK
office@jhpbooks.com
www.johnhuntpublishing.com
www.o-books.com

For distributor details and how to order please visit the 'Ordering' section on our website.

Text copyright: Barbara Berger 2021
Cover photo of the author: Søren Solkær
Front cover design: Tim Ray

ISBN: 978 1 78904 785 1
978 1 78904 786 8 (ebook)
Library of Congress Control Number: 2020950302

All rights reserved. Except for brief quotations in critical articles or reviews, no part of this
book may be reproduced in any manner without prior written permission from the publishers.

The rights of Barbara Berger as author have been asserted in accordance with the Copyright,
Designs and Patents Act 1988.

A CIP catalogue record for this book is available from the British Library.

Design: Stuart Davies

UK: Printed and bound by CPI Group (UK) Ltd, Croydon, CR0 4YY
Printed in North America by CPI GPS partners

We operate a distinctive and ethical publishing philosophy in
all areas of our business, from our global network of authors to
production and worldwide distribution.

With thanks

… to Tim Ray, I couldn't have done it without you.

Contents

Introduction: What Do Healthy Relationships Look Like?

Do you ever wonder what healthy relationships look like? Probably. Especially since most of the problems we have in our daily lives are "people problems" – have you noticed? Most of the difficulties we face on a daily basis have to do with our interactions with our fellow human beings. Be it with our partners, families, children, parents – or with our friends, neighbors or colleagues at work.

Take for example a challenging work situation. When we have problems, it's usually not because we don't have the required skill set to do our jobs, but rather our difficulties may be with a dominating boss or disrespectful coworkers. And we might face similar difficulties or problems on the home front, as we attempt to navigate through the challenges of getting along with our partners and children. And once again, it's not because we don't know how to cook, clean, make our beds or shop for food, but rather it's usually the challenge of how to deal with the other people that we are sharing this space with so there is a relative level of peace and harmony.

I know this is the biggest challenge for most people, not just from my own experience, but because I have worked for many years as a coach and therapist, so I have been hearing these problems over and over again every single day, year in and year out. And I hear people asking over and over again:

How can we get along with our fellow human beings?

How can we deal respectfully with our partners and families while still remaining true to who we are?

How can we manage better at the workplace - and deal with our superiors and colleagues so that we can maintain our self-respect and enjoy going to work?

In short, these questions boil down to:

What, in fact, do healthy relationships look like?

What are the characteristics and qualities of relationships that work and function for all the people involved?

How can we identify what works and what doesn't work?

This is what we all want to know.

And this is what this book is about. This book is an attempt to look realistically at these challenges and to answer these important questions.

Based on the way things are

In order to identify the characteristics that define healthy relationships – we must base our analysis on the reality of the way things are – and not on some dream or theoretical idea of how we think things "should" be. When we do this – when we look at reality – we quickly discover that people are different and that each person has his or her own background, thoughts, emotions and belief systems. Thus, each person also has his or her own interpretation of events, circumstances and people. In other words, when we look at reality, we discover that people are different and have different ideas about how things "should" be done.

So based on this reality – the reality that people are different and have different ideas about how to do things – how can we best get along with our fellow human beings? What do healthy relationships actually look like? What does a healthy relationship with a partner look like? What does a healthy family look like? How do parents relate to their children in a healthy manner? What are the characteristics of respectful, constructive conversations? How can we negotiate the challenges of our everyday lives and disagree respectfully with friends or family without running away or going on the attack? Is it possible to talk respectfully and find workable compromises?

I have discovered, from both my own personal journey as well as from my work as a coach and therapist for others, that most of us are rather confused when it comes to answering these very important questions.

The "Healthy Models" presented in this book are an attempt to answer these questions – based on the reality of how things are.

The value of Healthy Models

From my many years of clinical experience working with people, I have discovered that the value of these Healthy Models is that when we have a clear Model for how healthy behavior looks, people can then compare their own life situations and relationships to these Models and then identify what is "off" in their own experience.

For example, when we can define and clearly identify what healthy boundaries and respectful communications look like, it is easier for us to look at our own relationships and pinpoint where there might be a lack of healthy boundaries and respect.

Consequently, these Healthy Models help people to see, identify and pinpoint where there is unhealthy or disrespectful or "dysfunctional" behavior in their own relationships.

Most of the people who come to me for help can more or less articulate the fact that there is tension, unease, or real distress in some of their relationships. It could be with a partner or with family or friends, but what exactly is "off" and unhealthy is more problematic to pinpoint and define. They know they feel discomfort, but they don't know exactly what it is about or what has triggered it. But when they look at some of the Healthy Models presented in this book, people can then better identify where things are "off". They can begin to see where behavior is unhealthy and where there is, for example, a lack of respect or healthy boundaries. As a result, they begin to get a little more clarity – and are able to identify the situations or areas in their lives which are problematic. Which can be very helpful indeed, because then they can get to work on improving these situations.

So that is the value of these Healthy Models. They can help us identify what's going on and enable and empower us to work on improving these situations and relationships.

This book has 3 parts

Part 1: Healthy Models for Relationships: A presentation of the Healthy Models.

Part 2: Some Basic Observations About This Thing Called Life: A look at reality and the impersonal mechanisms and principles on which the Healthy Models are based.

Part 3: Healing Processes: A toolbox of processes and exercises we can use to deal with the consequences of relationships that have been less than healthy and respectful. Processes and exercises which are designed to help us identify, change and hopefully heal the emotional, psychological and physical damage caused by unhealthy relationships.

The power of repetition

Since we have all been programmed from birth with belief systems and thought patterns that are often out of alignment with "reality" – with the way things really are – reading this book and working with the Basic Observations and Healthy Models is a form of reprogramming and "re-wiring" of our consciousness. This is also why I often repeat the basic principles, concepts and Basic Observations. This is not a mistake but is done on purpose because repetition is an effective learning tool. When we keep on reading about and hearing and considering these concepts and Basic Observations from different angles and points of view, we gradually begin to learn and understand them and then they slowly become integrated into our thinking, and then finally, into our behavior. And that's when real change begins to happen in our lives.

Personal and clinical experience

As you will also discover, this book is written for both lay people and coaches and therapists. So sometimes in the presentation of a process or approach (especially in Part 3 of the book), I will refer to readers using a technique on their own at home and in other cases I may suggest working with a therapist or how a therapist might want to use a certain technique with a client.

And finally, everything I write about in this book is based on many years of clinical experience working with people – as well as my own personal experience and my own attempts to deal with the difficulties and challenges of my own family of origin as well as in my adult relationships. There is nothing in this book which I have not tried and tested on myself and with other people. But don't believe me. Read, consider, reread and try the material presented in this book for yourself. And see if it works for you. In my experience, it does!

Blessings to you on your journey!
Barbara Berger
Copenhagen, Denmark
April 2020

Part 1

Healthy Models for Relationships

Healthy Model No. 1

Basic Democratic Principles in Families and Other Close Relationships

To begin our exploration of Healthy Models for Relationships, let us start with one of the most fundamental and basic Healthy Models of all: Namely the principle and model of democracy. We all know what democracy is and what this principle means for the well-being of societies and the individuals who live in them. But what many of us unfortunately have not considered (or are unaware of) is that the principle of democracy is just as important to the health, happiness and well-being of our close relationships with our families, partners, and friends as it is to society in general.

Now what do I mean by that?

To begin with, let us first take a moment to briefly review the basic principles of democratic societies.

Every person has equal worth and rights

First and foremost, democratic societies are based on the recognition of the inherent worth or right to exist of each individual person. Each person, regardless of who he or she is, has the right to exist and be here. This is the basic principle of democracy. Thus in democratic societies, we have the principle of *one person one vote*. Every person has one vote. And one vote only – not more, nor less votes. Each member of our society has a right to their vote or voice, regardless. There is no high and low here. There are no conditions on this right to vote. A democratic society doesn't say you have to make so-and-so much money to have the right to vote. A democratic society doesn't say you can't vote when you are overweight or sick. Nor does it say you have to be beautiful or intelligent to vote. Each person has

9

a right to vote, regardless of their level of intelligence, their weight, their age, the amount of money they have in the bank, who they are married to, and so forth.

The basic principle in our democratic societies is that each individual has the right to be who she or he is and think whatever she or he thinks, as long as this person does not violate the rights of the next individual to think and live as she or he deems best.

For example, the Founding Fathers of the United States wrote about the basis of democracy as follows in 1776 in their Declaration of Independence:

We hold these truths to be self-evident, that all men are created equal, that they are endowed by their Creator with certain unalienable rights, that among these are life, liberty and the pursuit of happiness.

This is probably the clearest formulation of the foundation principle of democracy ever written.

Respect for the rights of the individual

Accordingly, because democratic societies are based on the idea of respecting each individual's right to live life as he or she deems best – this pristine right cannot be allowed to extend so far that one individual is able to interfere with or violate the rights of the next person or other people to live their lives as they deem best. This, of course, is the challenge of democracy. How do we achieve and maintain a system of governance that truly is based on the understanding that each individual is unique and has the right to live his or her life in the way that feels best to him or her – without interference from others?

In principle, all the laws in our democratic societies are attempts to regulate the interactions between individuals based on this concept of freedom so that we are able to respect the rights of others while attempting to live our lives in the way we each deem best. This, of course, can be very challenging to do at times, and this is also why we live in societies that are law-based. Our laws are an attempt to regulate the interactions between citizens as fairly and justly as possible. And to protect the rights of the individual.

In short, we can say – in a democratic society, you have the right to stand on your head all day long, if that's what feels best to you, as long as you don't interfere with my right to stand on my head all day long, if that's what feels best to me. So this freedom goes both ways; each one of us is allowed to live as freely and fully as possible as long as we respect the rights of our neighbors to live their lives as freely and fully as they can, and as they deem best.

How's democracy doing in our families and other close relationships?

Unfortunately, even though we live in so-called "democratic" societies, many people in families and couple relationships in practice neglect the basic principles of democracy when it comes to their respective family members, partners or children. If we take a closer look at what is actually going on in many families and couple relationships, we will see that often one or more of the people involved do not respect the rights of their respective family members or partners or children to have their say, to have their opinion, to disagree, to want different things – and/or in some cases to live their lives as they think and feel is best. All of which can greatly sabotage our ability to communicate, be close with each other, and enjoy all the many other wonderful benefits of human relationships.

But fortunately for us, there is a practical and effective way in which we can improve most of our relationships – and that is by applying the basic democratic principles to our relationships. Because when we do this, when we remind ourselves of these basic principles, we are then able to compare ourselves and our relationships to a Healthy Model for living sanely with other people (including those closest to us).

How does this look in practice?

Once we have reviewed the democratic principles mentioned above, we can then ask ourselves questions such as:

- Am I respecting the rights of the others in my family (or my partner) to have their say, to have their opinion, to disagree, to want different things – and to make their own choices (big and small) as to how they want to live their lives?
- Are the other members of this family (or my partner) respecting my right to have my say, to have my opinion, to disagree, to want different things – and to make my own choices (big and small) as to how I want to live my life?
- Is there an understanding in this family or in this relationship of the inherent worth of each one of us, even if we are different? In other words, regardless of gender, religion, sexual orientation, lifestyle, political choices, etc. – is there a basic respect for each person's right to be who they are and to be different from the way the other family members may be?
- When we are sharing the same living space or participating in the same activities, can we respectfully talk about and discuss the various ideas each one of us may have as to how we can best deal with whatever activities or situations we are participating in together?
- Can we understand and respect that we probably have different ideas as to how to deal with things? And as a result, are we willing to respectfully try to find "workable compromises" that all the involved parties can agree to? This is the way the legislative bodies in

democratic societies are designed to work in a well-functioning society. They try to find solutions (workable compromises) to the problems facing their societies. And to do this, they talk and discuss and debate and negotiate and, in the end, hopefully find workable compromises which then become legislation when the majority accepts and votes for these compromises/solutions. But the question here is, how well are we doing in terms of democracy and negotiating respectfully in our own homes and families?

We can be almost certain that there is a disregard for the basic democratic principles described above when members of a family (or one's partner) don't allow one of the people in the relationship to have his or her say, opinion, disagree, or want different things. Or when they try to pressure or manipulate this person into living life the way they believe is best for that individual. This is not only disrespectful and the cause of much stress, tension and disharmony in many families and relationships, it sadly shows a lack of understanding of the basic democratic principles upon which our societies are built. (These same problems – lack of basic respect for each person's right to be who he or she is – can unfortunately also be seen in close friendships and at the workplace.)

Once we understand that it's just as important to practice the basic democratic principles in our families, couple relationships and other close relationships as it is to practice them in our society in general, the question arises as to how these democratic principles actually play out in our relationships in practice. In other words, most specifically and concretely, how do we talk, act and treat each other when democratic principles and respect are our starting point? The Healthy Models that follow are all attempts to answer these important questions.

Healthy Model No. 2

The 3 Levels of Conversation

When we understand the basic democratic principles and the importance of respecting each individual's right to live and be who they are described in Healthy Model No. 1, we can then analyze the different types of conversations we have with the various people we interact with in our lives. When we have a clear Model of how healthy interactions take place, we can then also have a more realistic assessment of our conversations with people and then take the appropriate action to improve these relationships when adjustments are needed.

To help us analyze the various healthy interactions we can have with people, we can divide these interactions into three levels as follows:

Level 1: Respect and reasonable politeness
Level 2: Respect, reasonable politeness and polite interest
Level 3: Respect, reasonable politeness and genuine interest and appreciation

Let's look at the three levels:

Level 1: Respect and reasonable politeness

The first and most basic level of exchange between any two human beings is one where there is respect and ordinary politeness. We find this in our interactions when we go shopping or when we go to the dentist or doctor or the car repairman. These people don't have to be especially interested in us personally and we don't have to be especially interested in them personally, but we can interact politely because we have some kind of transaction that is important for both of us.

So again, respect and reasonable politeness are the basic elements here. You would never go back to a shop or to your dentist if the shopkeeper or dentist was aggressive or insulted you. So we rightfully expect this basic respect and politeness in these kinds of situations.

Level 2: Respect, reasonable politeness and polite interest

The next healthy level of exchange also involves respect and ordinary politeness as the basis of the exchange, but in these situations there is also polite interest. We often find these kinds of exchanges at the workplace. For example, you are sitting at a table in the canteen with some of your colleagues and everyone is talking about their recent vacations. Jack is talking about his skiing holiday in the Alps and you are not particularly interested in skiing, but you listen politely because he is your colleague and it's important that you get along well with each other. When Jack is done telling about his holiday, he asks you about yours. And since you spent the week shopping in Paris, you tell him what you did. He might not be particularly interested in Paris and shopping, but because he also wants to have a good working relationship with you, he listens politely to your tale. And so we have a normal, polite exchange without either party having to be especially interested in what the other person is saying or doing.

It is also important to note that in this type of healthy exchange, when things go well we are talking about a "dialogue" – and not a "monologue". In a healthy exchange, the one person tells his or her tale or ideas while the other person listens, and then the other person gets to say his or her bit while the other person listens. So there is a fair exchange. A conversation is "off-putting" when one person monopolizes the situation and talks constantly without allowing the other person to get a word in edgewise. Which means it is not a polite exchange. It is a "monologue" which the listener probably did not sign up for. This also indicates a basic lack of respect for one of the people involved.

Level 3: Respect, reasonable politeness and genuine interest and appreciation

In the third level of exchange, we not only have a reasonable level of politeness, we also have a genuine interest and feeling of appreciation. In this case, the two people involved are truly interested in each other and what they are doing. This, of course, is what happens between real friends and in good couple relationships. We have two or more people who are genuinely interested in each other and often passionately involved in hearing about and enjoying what the other person or people are up to.

Confusion about the levels of conversation

Firstly, it is important to remember and recognize that respect and a reasonable level of politeness (Level 1) are prerequisites for any type of interchange, regardless of which level of conversation we are talking about. When there is a lack of basic respect and reasonable politeness for your right to be you – stay away!

It is also very important to understand that there is often confusion about what kind of a relationship we are involved in, so we are often confused about what goes on. For example, most people "expect" their families to be genuinely interested in and appreciative of what they are doing (Level 3). Just because "we are family". This is a source of much confusion and discomfort or even anguish. In order to clear up this misunderstanding, it is important to understand that just because people are "family", it does not necessarily mean that they should be passionately or genuinely interested in what you are doing. Being family is no guarantee of that. Why? Because when we are realistic and understand that every person is unique, and that people are different, and have different backgrounds, interests, and different levels of consciousness (even though they are blood relatives or grew up in the same household), we can also understand that different people are interested in different things, regardless of whether or not they are family. So it is a good idea to remind ourselves that whether we are family or not, each person is living in their own mental universe. And that each person probably has, or often has, very different thoughts, feelings and emotions about what is going on, even if we grew up in the same family. That's just the way it is. So to expect your sister or father or brother or niece or nephew to take a passionate interest (Level 3) in the volunteer work you are doing just because you are "family" is probably not a good idea. But to expect basic respect and polite interest (Level 1 and 2), well again, this is a prerequisite for any type of exchange between you and other people, whether or not you are family.

The same goes for couple relationships. Your partner might not be genuinely interested in every little thing you do, but the very minimum required for an interaction is basic respect and a reasonable level of politeness. Without this, there is no platform for a healthy relationship.

In this connection, it is interesting to note that we often will accept or tolerate disrespectful types of behavior from our family members or partners (lack of Level 1: Respect and reasonable politeness) that we would never tolerate in a commercial exchange or from our friends. Just because we are "family", we somehow believe that disrespectful behavior is okay – but this is never the case! Ever!

So good questions to ask yourself about your various interactions with the people in your life would be:

- Am I respectful and polite when I meet other people, regardless of the situation and whether or not we are in agreement about things?

- And vice versa, do other people treat me with respect in the various interactions I have with others?
- Are there situations or interactions where there is a lack of basic respect and politeness?
- In terms of my family or my partner, do I overlook the importance of polite and respectful conversation because we are family or a couple?
- Do members of my own family or my partner overlook the importance of polite and respectful conversation because we are family or a couple?
- Do I need to work on my conversation skills? For more about improving your ability to communicate constructively, see Healthy Model No. 8: *Your Assertive Rights,* and Healthy Model No. 5: *It's Not What You Say – But How You Say It.*

The 4 Main Aspects of Good Couple Relationships (aka BB's Magic Formula for Good Couple Relationships)

Based on my many years of counseling people, I've identified what I call the four main areas which need to harmonize, more or less, for a couple relationship to continue and thrive:

1) *Good sex*
2) *Good energy when you're together*
3) *Shared values and interests*
4) *Respect (especially when you are not in agreement)*

Let's look at these four areas and see why they are so important. But before we start, I'd like to emphasize that we're not talking about two people always matching 100% in each of these areas, but that on the whole, the two of you should be more or less a good match in these four areas.

1) Good sex

I start with good sex because for most of us, our relationships begin with the excitement of meeting and with the good sex. It's fun and we feel good about it. So sex is a weathervane in any relationship, even after people have been together for a while. So how is your sex life? Are you still doing it? How often? Does it feel good? Is it a source of pleasure in your relationship or a source of tension and disappointment? Or has it just sort of faded into the distance...

2) Good energy when you're together

By this I mean that when the two of you are together, is there good energy? More or less, most of the time? In other words, does it feel good when you're together? Is there a relaxed and lighthearted atmosphere when you are together even though each of you is doing your own thing? And what about when you're doing stuff together – is there good energy? Or is it just a drag? Or is there a lot of tension, irritation, or bad feelings? How does it really feel when you're together. Be honest.

3) Shared values and interests

Shared values and interests are another important area where people need to be more or less in harmony for a couple relationship to work in the long run. And by this I mean, even if you love each other, if the one person wants to spend all their time meditating on a mountaintop in silence while the other person wants to spend all their time shopping in Paris or London, you might not be such a good match because what are you going to do together? You don't like to hang out the way he/she likes to hang out, and he/she doesn't like to hang out the way you do. So again, it's important that people have at least some shared interests if they want to do stuff together and hang out. So it's nice if both parties like to go skiing or like to go hiking or camping or walking in the mountains or lazing on the beach. Or if both parties love going to the theater or to the movies and concerts. Because it's fun and important to have things we can do together and really enjoy doing together.

Shared values are also very important. Again, if one partner wants to have an open relationship and wants to have sex with multiple partners, while the other person wants a monogamous relationship – then it can be hard to live together harmoniously because you don't have shared values. It's not that one way or the other is "right" or "wrong", but rather that the two of you are probably just too far away from each other to live together harmoniously. I always say if two consenting adults want to be chained together from morning to evening every day of the week – and they agree that this works for them – well fine! And if two consenting adults say they want to live apart and meet only once a month and bonk for 24-hours nonstop – and they agree that this works for them – well fine! So we're not talking about "right" or "wrong" here, we're just talking about finding what works for two people.

Other shared values which can be important in couple relationships are, for example, having kids. It can be a problem if one of you wants to have kids and the other doesn't. How is that going to work? Or what about if you do have children; then there is the question of how to bring them up. If the one parent goes in for very strict discipline and the other parent is more laid-back, this again can create disagreement and tension in terms of how to bring up children. Who gets to decide?

And what about keeping the house clean? I have seen the same problem arise in couples here when it comes to the level of tidiness. If the one person is very neat and tidy and the other is very messy, this again can cause endless problems and tension when these two people are living together in the same space.

So shared values are not so much a question of "right" or "wrong", but rather a question of how much in alignment two people are with each other when it comes to being together and/ or living together and sharing the same space. Is there some form of agreement about some of the basic activities these two people are sharing in the relationship? Because when the distance between the two parties is too great, when two people are too far apart in their basic approaches to life and the various everyday issues we face, it can make being together and/or living together very challenging.

4) Respect (especially when you are not in agreement)

Respect is my final point and is probably the most important of them all. By respect I mean, can you and do you treat each other with respect – especially when you disagree about things! It's easy to be nice and treat your partner respectfully if you always agree with each other. But are you psychologically mature enough to understand and realize that even people who love each other can disagree with each other. And sometimes often do! Do you understand that this is because we are all different and all have different backgrounds and ideas about how things should be and what to do. For a relationship to work, it's vitally important to understand that love and agreement are two different things. We can love someone very much and still disagree with them. So treating each other with respect, especially when you disagree with each other, is the most crucial aspect of any good relationship. Because if you can do this, if you can respectfully listen to each other and then sit down and discuss ways in which you can reach a workable compromise on whatever issues you find challenging, then your relationship has a really good chance of not just surviving, but of thriving!

How respect affects all the areas

When you look at your relationship (or previous relationships, which can be an interesting exercise) in the light of these four areas, you will probably notice that you and your partner are stronger in some areas than in others. But regardless, using these four points as markers will make it easier for you to identify where the strengths and weaknesses in your relationship are and what steps (if any) you can take to improve things.

You will also see that especially when you work on point 4 – Respect – and develop or improve respectful ways of communicating when there are disagreements (there is much more about how to communicate constructively in this book), it influences the energy between you and automatically there is better energy when you are together (point 2). This also often makes your sex life better too (point 1). So it all hangs together! And the better it gets, the better it gets.

Friendship, business partnerships and other close working relationships

It's also interesting to note that if we remove point 1 (good sex) and just consider the 3 remaining points – good energy when you're together, shared values and interests, and respect – we end up with the three areas that have to be more or less in harmony for almost any other close relationship to function and thrive. And this holds true whether we are talking about close friendships, business partnerships, or any other type of close working or creative partnership. Thus, if there are problems or bad energy in any of these types of close relationships, we can use these points as markers to help us identify where things are off course and what steps we need to take to remedy them.

Healthy Model No. 4

Rights and Responsibilities in Relationships

RIGHTS AND RESPONSIBILITIES

Healthy relationships are democracy in action.
Adults/friends/family members/colleagues/
couples/parents, etc.
together make joint agreements
concerning joint activities, projects, the home, children, etc.

Rights	Responsibilities
You have a right to be you.	You are to respect other people's right to be who they are.
You have a right to have all your thoughts and feelings.	You are to respect that other people have the right to have all their thoughts and feelings.
You have a right to have your opinions about everything.	You are to respect that other people have the right to have their opinions about everything.
You are to be treated with respect.	You are to treat other people with respect.
	You are to respect the agreements you make with other people.

Agreements (between partners, friends, in families, with colleagues) concerning for example:
Joint projects
Living together
Working together
Having children together, etc.

Healthy Model No. 5

It's Not *What* You Say – But *How* You Say It

To further explore how we can better relate to our fellow human beings, it can also help to examine the ways in which we communicate with each other. When we do this, we can more easily identify and understand how we can communicate more constructively and skillfully. To do this, it can help to understand that there are two distinctly different aspects to all our communications. These two aspects are:

1) *What we are talking about or communicating about (the specific subject matter or topic)*
2) *The way in which we are talking or communicating*

These are the two distinctly different aspects of all communications. There's the specific topic or subject itself and then there is the way in which it is communicated. So let's examine this mechanism.

1) What we are talking about or communicating about (the specific subject matter or topic)

So to start with, it's important to understand that the reality is that there are a million, billion different things, topics, and subjects that we human beings can talk about. We can talk about almost everything and anything under the sun – and we do. For example: politics, sex, family, food, the environment, sports, clothes, money, movies, children, work – you name it. Moreover, when we have a more mature and realistic understanding of the human condition and the nature of this thing called life, we can also see that we, human beings, can disagree, and often do, about almost everything that we can possibly find to talk about. That's just the way things are. That's the reality. People disagree about things all the time. And the fact that we often disagree arises because every human being is different and unique. Each and every one of us is having our own completely unique experience of this thing called Life, based on our own specific background, upbringing and programming. Which is why we can also understand that even in the exact same situation, different people will be having very different reactions, experiences, and very different opinions about the exact same event or circumstance. This is because each person has his or her own way of relating to whatever is going on, based on their background, thoughts and belief systems. (For more about this mechanism, see the Basic Observations in Part 2 of this book.)

When we understand this (the diversity of human life), we can also understand that it is not very realistic to expect that we, human beings, always should agree about a lot of things. Rather it is a lot more sane and healthy to expect disagreement – and then learn how to navigate wisely in our interactions with other people based on this reality. This is what I call "getting real" about being a human being. Getting real is understanding that we are all different and that we are probably going to disagree about a lot of things. But this doesn't mean we can't live together in relative peace and harmony, especially if we understand the basic mechanisms of good communications.

So it is vitally important to understand that yes, there are a million different topics we can talk about and there can be a million different opinions about each topic – *BUT then there is also the way in which we talk to each other. There are respectful ways of talking and communicating with our fellow human beings and there are disrespectful ways.* Which is why it is crucial to understand that there is a difference between *what* we say and *how* we say it.

2) The way in which we are talking or communicating

So let's look at the ways in which we speak to each other about all the millions of different topics we may be speaking together about.

What do I mean by the various ways in which we speak to each other? I mean, for example, regardless of the subject matter, what kind of language are we using? Are the words that we are using respectful or disrespectful towards the person/people we are talking to? Does our language show or demonstrate that we are listening to and recognizing the other person's right to their opinions and belief? Our language tells a lot about our level of respect and openness. Moreover, what about our tone of voice? Is it moderate and pleasant or is it loud and aggressive? Are we calling the person names? (This involves both the words and the tone of voice.) Are we using curse words? (Again words and tone of voice.) Once more, it is important to understand that our tone of voice communicates so much about the level of respect we have for the other person/people involved.

Here are two examples of the different ways we can say the same thing:

Example 1: Jane would like to go for an evening walk with her husband, Bill, who's watching TV. How does Jane communicate her desire to him?

- **Disrespectful:** *You never want to do anything with me. All you do is sit there and watch those stupid programs every evening! Why can't we just go for a walk?*
- **Respectful:** *What a beautiful evening it is tonight. Would you like to go for a walk with me down to the lake? I'd really like you to go with me.*

Example 2: Maggie and her new boyfriend, Jack, get invited

to brunch in town on Sunday by a group of Maggie's friends. Maggie really wants to go with Jack and show him off to all her friends, but he doesn't seem interested. So she asks him again if he will go with her. How will Jack answer Maggie if he doesn't want to go?

- **Disrespectful:** *Hell no, how many times do I have to tell you? I don't want to go to that damn brunch with all your friends. I won't know a soul and it will be such a bore. So will you stop pestering me?*
- **Respectful:** *I am sure it will be really fun for you, Maggie, but I won't know a soul, and to be honest, I'd rather just chill out for a couple of hours on my own on Sunday. I've got a really busy week at work coming up next week.*

As you can see from the above, it was the same message both times, but the ways the messages were delivered were vastly different.

Another important aspect to consider is our body language. How is that? Are we relaxed and open or tense and angry? It is important to recognize that our body language always sends a strong and clear message to the people we are communicating with (whether we like it or not). Plus there is our overall energy – the energy we are sending out. Is our energy pleasant, relaxed and inviting or are we feeling defensive or aggressive? Does our energy convey that we are open to discussion and that we honestly believe we can find a workable compromise if we are discussing something where we both are involved?

And what about the people you are speaking to and with? How are they talking to you? Is the person you are speaking with respectful or disrespectful? What about his or her tone of voice? Is it friendly and relaxed or angry and aggressive? And what about his or her body language? Choice of words? What kind of energy is this person sending your way? Do you feel relaxed or intimidated by this person? And why?

These are all very important questions to consider and ask ourselves if we are genuinely interested in understanding and improving our ability to communicate. And also, if we are trying to understand what has happened or is happening in our various interactions with other people. If you watch what is going on, you will notice that some people are just easier to talk to – whether or not you happen to be in agreement about things. They are just more relaxed, respectful and open to discussion. They don't all the time act as if they have to prove they are right. They are more mature psychologically and understand that people have different opinions and ideas, and that it's not so challenging or dangerous to their well-being if we disagree. Plus they can tolerate the fact that sometimes, or even often, other people will not understand them or agree with them. So again just notice. Watch what's going on. By watching your interactions and then analyzing them based on the various observations from this book, you will learn so much about the art of communicating. And you will see more and more clearly what works and what obviously doesn't.

When you have this key – that there is a difference between the subject matter you are talking about and the way in which you speak – you also have the key to improving your ability to communicate with almost everyone you meet. Then you can begin to understand that there are many ways of saying the exact same thing. When you understand this, you will also find that you can, in fact, talk about almost everything. You can even talk about things that may be unpleasant or controversial to the other person/people, if you know how to present your ideas diplomatically and skillfully. In this connection, I highly recommend listening to interviews with great world leaders and good communicators such as the Dalai Lama or Barack Obama to see how inclusive and all-embracing these great communicators are when it comes to talking about controversial subjects.

They almost always frame their remarks or ideas with general statements like: "This is a very complicated issue. There are no easy answers. Humanity has been struggling with this matter for generations. But I believe if we can all sit down together and discuss the matter, we can probably find some answers or workable compromises." So again, great communicators often frame their ideas by showing their genuine interest in communicating openly and honestly with other people. They are generally inclusive and respectful. So we are talking "good human qualities" here. Learning to listen respectfully and then communicating our thoughts and ideas as skillfully as we possibly can.

Healthy Model No. 6

You Have Inherent Worth

Understanding that you have inherent worth, no matter who you are or what you are doing, is fundamental to being at peace with yourself and living a good life. This is why it is so important to recognize – when looking at or contemplating our value or worth as human beings – that there is a big difference between our inherent worth and our performance in life and on the world stage.

Many people – especially those with low self-esteem or with inflated self-esteem (or low self-confidence or inflated self-confidence) – do not understand this difference. Regardless of whether this low or inflated self-esteem is expressed in the form of shyness and insecurity or as boastfulness and bragging, both types of behavior are indicators of misunderstood self-esteem. The one type (low self-esteem) is projected inward because it is based on the idea that there is something wrong with me or that I am worth less than others. The other type (inflated self-esteem) is projected outward because it is based on the idea that I am better than others. In either case, there is a basic and fundamental misunderstanding of the fact that every person alive has equal inherent worth.

So let's look a little more closely at the difference between inherent worth and a person's ability to perform (his or her performance) in different areas of his or her life.

Inherent worth

To begin with, what do I mean by inherent worth? Inherent worth is a characteristic of Life itself, which is why each person has inherent worth. Because each person is alive, each one of us is an expression of, or an individualization of, Life or the

Life Force or the energy of Life. Thus, Life or inherent worth are actually synonymous. Life or inherent worth is something we have, something we are born with, something that can't be added to or subtracted from. It is something that just is. So when we talk about inherent worth, we are talking about the mysterious quality of Life itself. And because this Life that we have is a given, so is inherent worth. It's something we all are and have or we wouldn't be here. So inherent worth is innate, inborn; it is all about existence itself.

Thus, we see that inherent worth is really a "spiritual" or "metaphysical" or "existential" truth or reality because Life is what we are to begin with. This pre-given condition is not something we can earn or get more of. Nor is it possible to have less inherent worth or lose it. Consequently, we see that inherent worth actually describes the inbuilt pristine nature of existence itself. This is the indestructible core of you and me, which is Life itself. Moreover, whether we are in these bodies or not, whatever form Life itself takes, Life continues, indestructible. Everyone can see this. All we have to do is look around. Everywhere we look, we can see there is Life or existence. Only the form nature of existence changes. This is a wonderful thing to meditate upon. That we are Life itself and that this is why we all have inherent worth. It's truly a metaphysical, existential, and deeply spiritual concept.

The difference between inherent worth and our ability to perform

In addition to our inherent worth, there is our performance or our ability to perform and do stuff in the world. By this I mean, the things you and I do or can do. You could call this our expertise, our activities, the skills we have. And these skills or activities vary from person to person, from situation to situation, from age group to age group, from culture to culture. But each one of us has certain areas where we are stronger and certain areas where we are not as strong. In addition, almost everyone learns some skills in school or at home or from somewhere along their pathway in life, which they may or may not be using to earn a living or as their chosen career path. But this has nothing to do with a person's inherent worth. Inherent worth, as I said above, is a given, something each person is endowed with – because we all have been given the gift of Life. Unfortunately, the confusion arises for many of us because in our society, we learn (or have been programmed) from an early age to judge people by what they do or what they have or what they have achieved in the world. For example, we learn to judge people by how much money they make, or how much success they have, or how they look, or who they are married to, or how many children they have, or how much they weigh. Thus, we train each other, or program each other, to believe that our value has something to do with what we have or can do – with our performance, with our career path, with the amount of money we make, with our looks, our weight, or who we are married to. The list of outer conditions and circumstances we may be using when judging each other can be incredibly long. And this can be very stressful for most of us, especially if we often compare ourselves to other people and measure our "value" or "worth" in terms of what we do or have, compared to other people. When this happens, it is not hard to understand why so many people may be feeling unworthy or not good enough.

This is not to say we cannot strive to improve ourselves or to learn new skills. Of course, we can. Nor is this meant to, in any way, denigrate the fact that, yes, one person is indeed a renowned brain surgeon, and another is a leading expert in computer science or engineering or literature or languages or art or design. But this kind of expertise – whatever it is – has nothing to do with a person's "worth". Which is why this distinction is something we must beware of.

Inherent worth and democracy

This is also why it is so important to go back to and remind ourselves of the basic principles that our democratic societies are built on. The most basic principle of all is this understanding of, and respect for, each person's inherent worth. This idea and understanding that each individual is a unique creation of Life itself is fundamental to our idea of democracy. And this, of course, is the big difference between dictatorship and democracy. Democracies understand and value each individual's right to life and liberty. Whereas dictatorships do not because when power is in the hands of one individual or a few individuals, there is no respect for the inherent worth of each human being.

This is also why in a democracy, each individual has one vote, because each individual has an inherent right to have his or her say in matters, regardless of what he or she does or his or her social status. Thus, the individual's right to have a say is based on the concept of the pristine inherent worth of each human being and is not dependent on his or her status in society or achievements. In theory, none of these qualities should make any difference in democracies which are built on the recognition of each person's inherent worth. And as a result, each individual has one vote. No one person's vote is more important than another's.

Hence, we can see that democracy is based on understanding that each individual has a right to his or her say because each individual has inherent worth. And most fundamentally, each individual has inherent worth because each individual is an expression of Life itself.

Therefore I suggest that if you want to live more happily and feel more comfortable and secure in being who you are, you consider these things and remind yourself over and over again that inherent worth and a person's ability to perform in the world are two very different things.

Inherent worth has nothing to do with who you are or how

successful you are. You have inherent worth, regardless.

Inherent worth versus performance-based worth

Inherent worth is independent of all conditions (none of the below matters or is relevant)

Different types of performance-based worth

As people evolve, their idea of performance-based worth evolves too. As shown below.

Higher levels of consciousness
↑
Judging people by who they are → performance-based worth
↑
Judging people by what they do → performance-based worth
↑
Judging people by what they have → performance-based worth
↑
Lower levels of consciousness

Healthy Model No. 7

You Have an Inner Compass

Not only do you have inherent worth, you also have an Inner Compass. Yes, it's true. You have your own personal, internal guidance system that is working all the time and which is constantly giving you precise and reliable guidance and information as to what is best for you and whether or not you are in alignment with who you truly are. Your internal guidance system is also letting you know if you are living in healthy, respectful relationships. I call this internal guidance system – the Inner Compass.

So how does your Inner Compass give you this guidance? It does so by means of your emotions. Your emotions are the way in which your Inner Compass lets you know whether or not you are in alignment with who you truly are and if you are on the right track for you. The way the Inner Compass works is like this: When you feel good, when you feel a sense of aliveness and ease and flow in your life, when you feel passion, joy or enthusiasm, these good-feeling emotions are all indicators that you are in alignment with who you really are. These emotions mean that you are on the right track for you, and living in healthy, respectful relationships. When you feel less than good, when you feel a sense of discomfort or are anxious or unhappy or distressed in any way, these negative emotions are indicators that you are out of alignment and not doing what's best for you. Which could mean, for example, that some of your relationships or interactions with other people are not respectful and healthy. In other words, you're off track...

Your direct connection to the Great Universal Intelligence

The Inner Compass is a very simple, but powerful mechanism. It is an internal yes/no mechanism that is your direct connection to the Great Universal Intelligence – that Greater Intelligence that created this amazing Universe and all Life in it, including you. In order to provide you with a clear indication of whether or not you are in alignment with what the Greater Intelligence knows to be the truth about you, the Inner Compass works like the North/South guidance of an ordinary directional compass. When you are in alignment – when you are living in harmony with who you truly are and what is best for you – your Inner Compass points directly North and you feel a sense of comfort, ease and flow in your life. In other words, you feel good. And when you're not in alignment with who you truly are (with the North/South position), it means you are off course, and as a result, you feel a sense of discomfort or unease. In other words, you don't feel so good. It's as simple as that.

But unfortunately, so many of us have lost touch with our inbuilt internal guidance system. Firstly because no one ever told us about the Inner Compass. And secondly because we have been programmed from an early age to listen to others and seek the love and approval of other people rather than trusting our own sense of what feels right to us. As a result, we don't even know that each one of us has his, or her, own personal, internal guidance system, nor do we realize that this is what our emotions are all about. We don't understand the true significance of our emotions. In other words, we don't realize that our emotions are actually signals from within, which are all the time telling us whether or not we are in alignment with the Great Universal Intelligence and who we truly are – and with what is best for us, in every given moment in time or situation.

How did I discover this mechanism?

I discovered that each one of us has an Inner Compass because whenever I looked around, I found I could observe the amazing intelligence of the greater web of Life of which we are all a part. I could see how the planets rotate around the sun in perfect harmony and how the sun comes up every morning and how the plants grow and the animals appear and multiply and how the babies are born. And I could also see that all this is happening all by itself, because obviously it's not something that you or I are doing. So I realized that there is a greater intelligence that is actually running this amazing show of Life in which we are all participating. And to simplify matters, I decided to call this All-Present Intelligence, the Great Universal Intelligence. That Greater Intelligence which is doing all of this – which is manifesting the Universe and all of Life, including you and me.

Here's how you can confirm for yourself that there is some Greater Intelligence doing all this. Just look at yourself and notice that you are here in this body. That is something you can see for yourself. But in truth, you can't honestly say that you created your body, can you? Nevertheless, your heart beats all by itself and your food gets digested and your lungs just breathe – all by themselves. So again, there must be a Greater Intelligence that created you and that has manifested as the intelligence of your cells, organs and body. And since this Greater Intelligence created you and is animating you right now, this must also mean that this Greater Intelligence is in you and that you are connected to it. And this connection is what I call your Inner Compass. Your Inner Compass is your direct link to this Greater Intelligence, which created all of Life, including you.

An important discovery

This is why learning about the Inner Compass is such an amazing and important discovery. Because it is our direct, personal connection to the Great Universal Intelligence, that intelligence which is far, far beyond our own individual ability to see, understand and analyze all the information and data that is always available in the vastness of this infinite Universe at any given moment in time. In addition, the discovery of the Inner Compass is so important because when we realize we have this internal guidance system, we can also better understand that our emotions really do matter – in ways we did not comprehend before. So we come to realize that how we feel matters because these emotions are signals from this Greater Intelligence.

And yes of course, we all know we have emotions. Everyone knows when something feels good or bad, everyone knows the difference between feeling angry and feeling love, between feeling depressed and feeling joyful... but what most of us still don't understand or realize is that these emotions are important indicators from within because they are giving us vital information about whether or not we are in alignment with the Great Universal Intelligence and who we truly are.

As a result, because this understanding of the Inner Compass has been lost, we don't realize that our emotions are the key to understanding and using our own personal internal guidance system. But the good news is that once we rediscover this mechanism and understand its importance, we can learn to use our Inner Compass again. All it requires is the willingness to take the time to notice the signals we are receiving from within and then try to adjust (little by little) our thinking and behavior so that we are moving in the direction of what gives us more and more of a sense of ease and flow.

The Inner Compass exercise

So how can you start working with this new understanding?

To help you start getting in touch with your Inner Compass on a daily basis, I have developed what I call the Inner Compass exercise.

Here's what to do:

First of all, remind yourself that you have an Inner Compass and think about what this actually means. Reread this Healthy Model again or read my book *Find and Follow Your Inner Compass – Instant Guidance in an Age of Information Overload*, which gives an in-depth description of the Inner Compass mechanism.

Then make up your mind to start noticing how you actually feel, really honestly feel, at various times during the course of your day.

Notice when things feel good and notice when they don't. (This is not about how you think you "should" feel. This is about being honest about how you actually do feel.) Notice when you feel good and when you don't.

In addition, when you notice during the course of your day that you are thinking more about what other people may be thinking or feeling about you – or about a situation, person, or event than you are – immediately pull back your focus from speculating about what other people may be thinking or feeling and return your focus to yourself. This means when you catch yourself worrying about what your boss or partner or mother or friends may be thinking, just drop it. Drop it like a hot potato! Stop trying to figure out what other people may or may not be thinking or feeling or wanting – and return your attention to what's going on inside you. Notice what your Inner Compass is telling you by means of your emotions about whatever is going on. Take a moment and notice how it feels. That's all there is to it.

I know this sounds very simple, but as simple as this may sound, it's not that easy for most people to do. Because we have been programmed and trained most of our lives to focus on other people and to please them. Most of us have learned from a very early age to try to tune ourselves into what other people want and need so we don't know how to tune into our Inner Compass anymore. This is why when trying this exercise, it will feel rather strange in the beginning, because we have become so used to focusing our attention away from ourselves and on others. It will feel odd to stop focusing on other people and turn our attention back to ourselves.

But this is what using your Inner Compass is about: Turning your attention away from other people and focusing on yourself.

Now to summarize, here are the main points of the exercise plus a few other important pointers that will help strengthen your ability to hear and follow your own internal guidance system:

1) Understand that you have an Inner Compass that is giving you information at all times – via your feelings – about what is best for you. The better something feels, the more ease and flow you are experiencing, the more it is a signal from your Inner Compass that this is the way forward for you. The more uncomfortable something feels, the more it is a signal from your Inner Compass that this is not the way for you.

2) Check your Inner Compass regularly. Stop every so often during the course of your day and notice what kind of impulses you are receiving from your Inner Compass. Ask yourself: What feels good right now? In what direction do I feel the most flow and good energy?

3) If noticing how you really feel about people and situations is new to you, just start slowly and notice. Don't feel that you immediately have to take action on what you discover. Just notice. Try to be honest with yourself.

4) As you begin to get used to noticing the signals from your Inner Compass, you will discover that you automatically begin to make small adjustments or changes in your life. This just happens naturally. It's not something you have to force.

5) Remind yourself that even though other people mean well, they don't have access to your Inner Compass. Only you do. When you notice that you are thinking or worrying about what other people are perhaps thinking – drop it like a hot potato! And return your attention to what's going on inside you and just notice how you really feel.

6) Also as we learn to listen to and follow our Inner Compass, it does not mean we should not treat our fellow human beings with respect. Of course, we should!

7) It is also important to understand: The better you feel, the more ease and flow and good energy you experience, the greater your capacity to support the other people in your life. The more stressed and overwhelmed you are, the more difficult it is for you to support the people in your life. So even though some might say following your Inner Compass is a selfish thing to do, the reality is that it's also the best thing you can do if you want to support others and make a positive contribution to the world.

8) There is no universal standard – no one size fits all. What feels good to you (to your Inner Compass) might not feel so good to someone else (to their Inner Compass). Because we are all different, each one of us is unique, and we are all at different places in our lives and at different stages of our development.

9) Mind your own business. Remember and respect the fact that everyone – every person you know – also has an Inner Compass that is giving them information about what's best for them.

What if someone disapproves?

But what if your Inner Compass guides you in the direction of something that goes against the wishes, ideas, preferences or opinions of your partner or family or friends or colleagues? What do you do then? How do you navigate wisely in situations like this? How can you honor both your relationships with the other important people in your life while at the same time staying in alignment with your own integrity (the Inner Compass)? Since the fear of disapproval and trying to please other people are among the main obstacles to following our Inner Compass, this can truly be a great challenge.

To meet this challenge, we must learn how to be assertive, communicate constructively and respectfully, and have healthy boundaries. In the next Healthy Models of this book, we will take a closer look at these healthy and respectful ways of interacting with our fellow human beings.

Healthy Model No. 8

Your Assertive Rights – You Have the Right to Say No

Since the fear of disapproval and trying to please other people are among the main obstacles to being true to ourselves and following our Inner Compass, let's take a closer look at these phenomena.

But before we start, let me say most emphatically that when I talk about pleasing others, I am not saying you should not treat other people with respect. And I am not saying you should not support your friends and family in their endeavors. Nor am I saying you should not be a kind, compassionate human being.

What I am talking about is when we say or do things which go against our own integrity (our Inner Compass) because we want to please someone else or because we are afraid of their disapproval. I am talking about situations and activities where we disregard our integrity and go against the voice within us because we are afraid of criticism or rejection. It could be in relation to our partner, our parents, our children, our friends – the list of possible people we believe we can displease is often quite long!

One of the main elements behind our fear of displeasing others is the prevalent belief that we are somehow responsible for the happiness (or unhappiness) of other people. This translates into the belief that if you or I do what feels right to us (and as a consequence don't do what someone else wants us to do) – then that person will be unhappy. And if they are unhappy, it's our fault! So consciously or unconsciously, most of us have been programmed from an early age to link the happiness and well-being of other people to what we say and do (or don't say and do). But can this be true? Can we actually be responsible for how another person thinks or feels? Can your choices or mine make another person happy or unhappy?

In order to answer this very important question, we have to go back to the Nature of Reality and examine the actual setup of this life experience. Because when we do, we will see that we cannot possibly be responsible for another person's reactions to what we say or do (or don't say or do). Because each individual's experience is determined by this person's own thoughts and beliefs, and how he or she relates to what is going on in his or her life. For a detailed exploration of the basic mechanisms that govern how each person reacts and experiences life, see Part 2 of this book. Here I describe in detail how each person's thinking and belief systems determine their experience as well as who is responsible for whose experiences.

Arbitrary standards of behavior

When people try to pressure you into doing what they want you to do (typically because they consciously or unconsciously believe that getting you to do what they want will make them feel better), they usually don't do this by saying directly, "My happiness depends on you! If you don't do what I want, I'll be miserable." (Although some people actually do say this outright!) Most people will instead try to get you to do what they want by appealing to some higher standard of behavior, some arbitrary standard of "right" and "wrong" to justify their request.

They will either say or imply that, "This is simply how we do things" in our family, in our country, in the Western world, if we're good Christians, if we're good Jews, if we're good Muslims, etc., etc. What is implied here is that there is some higher standard involved that we have either forgotten, overlooked or don't quite have the intelligence to figure out for ourselves! In other words, there is some higher standard that is more important than any silly ideas you or I might have as to what feels best to us.

This, unfortunately, has been the case for most of us. From early childhood, most of us have been trained/manipulated by our parents, teachers, friends and others (all with good intentions of course) who have tried to control our behavior by appealing to arbitrary universal standards of right and wrong. Standards which many of us have never quite figured out or understood. But whether or not we understood them, from childhood on, it has been implied that there are some higher standards, which we in our imperfection need to follow. And since we're not bright enough to figure this out for ourselves, we need to be controlled and corralled into place by other people (who seemingly know more than we do) who can point out to us the inappropriateness of our behavior. And they do this by telling us that our behavior is either improper, indecent, immoral or somehow unacceptable because it doesn't match the standard they're going by (whatever that happens to be).

People who use tactics like this may include our mothers, fathers, sisters, brothers, partners, other family members, our children, cousins, neighbors, people at work – you name it. There are people like this everywhere you turn. But in most cases, it is usually someone who is not good at simply asking for what they want – for example by saying – "I would prefer if you'd…" or, "I'd really like you to…" and who is then unable to respect your answer. Instead, non-assertive people like this try to manipulate you into doing what they want by appealing to some higher, arbitrary standard of perfection that they say you are not living up to.

Unfortunately for us, the consequence of all this is that if we ourselves actually do believe there really are some higher, arbitrary standards of right and wrong out there that are better able to determine what is right or wrong for us than we are, then we're easy targets for other people to manipulate… which also makes it difficult to look within and follow our integrity and listen to the signals from our Inner Compass.

(For more about arbitrary standards and how to avoid being manipulated by them, see my books *Are You Happy Now? 10 Ways to Live a Happy Life* and *Find and Follow Your Inner Compass – Instant Guidance in an Age of Information Overload*.)

What about family, partners, friends?

So what if your Inner Compass (integrity) tells you to do something that goes against the wishes of your family or partner or friends and colleagues? What then? What do you do? Give up your dream? Don't listen to your Inner Compass (integrity)? Grit your teeth and get on with the plans of other people for you and your life?

It's a good question isn't it? And this is where so many people get into trouble even if they know in their heart of hearts what feels best to them and what they really want to do. It could be, for example, choosing a career track our family or friends don't approve of, or being in a same sex relationship, or marrying someone of a different race or religion, or dropping out of school or going back to school, or changing jobs or quitting your job or... the list of things you might want to do that your family, partner or friends might disapprove of is endless. (It all depends on their belief systems.)

So what can you do?

If you don't want to give up your right to be you and make your own decisions, this is when it's important to remind yourself that you have a right to be you and that you have an Inner Compass, which is always giving you reliable guidance as to what is best for you. And remember, even if your family or friends have forgotten, we are all fortunate enough to be living in democratic societies which are designed to protect the rights of the individual to live the life that he or she chooses. (For more about democracy and basic democratic principles, see Healthy Model No. 1.) Therefore, if you are in doubt, think upon these things over and over again until you are sure you understand the basic principles of democracy and human behavior. Remind yourself that it's not your job to make other people happy (it's their job). For more about making other people happy or unhappy, see Part 2 of this book. And finally, remember that it is your job to follow your integrity and support everyone else in following theirs.

When we understand this, we are still left with the big question: What to do when your integrity or Inner Compass guides you to make decisions or go in a direction that some of the people in your life might dislike or disapprove of? What happens if you have been programmed to seek the love and approval of other people, while at the same time you are being guided to move in a direction that might trigger someone's disapproval?

This is where understanding our Assertive Rights and assertiveness training come into the picture.

Assertiveness training and constructive communications

Why assertive rights and assertiveness training? Because if you're in a situation where other people disagree with you or your choices or projects, it's important to know how to take care of yourself, set healthy boundaries, and say no in a respectful manner when something doesn't feel right to you. This is what being assertive is all about. Being assertive means that you can take care of yourself when other people interfere with your right to be you and make the decisions which feel best to you.

The good news is that when we learn to be assertive in a constructive and respectful manner, it actually makes it much easier for each one of us to follow our integrity. Because then we know that we can take care of ourselves when we are guided to do something that the people around us might not approve of.

Nothing helps reduce anxiety like assertiveness training.

In addition, it's important to understand (and then to keep reminding ourselves) that being assertive is something most of us must learn to do and practice doing. It's usually not something we learned at home when we were children. Quite the contrary, because even though most children are naturally assertive when they are small, this natural assertiveness has usually been programmed (or pounded) out of us at an early age as our parents and teachers trained us to do what they wanted us to do instead of following our own inner guidance. So unfortunately, learning to be assertive as adults doesn't just happen overnight. It is something we have to relearn and practice.

So let's take a very brief look at what it means to be assertive and some of the things you can learn to do when other people are trying to persuade you, pressure you or manipulate you into doing what they want you to do.

Your assertive rights

When it comes to learning to be assertive, a good place to begin is to read and think about the list of assertive rights below that were mapped out by Manuel J. Smith in his classic assertiveness book *When I Say No, I Feel Guilty.*

Your assertive rights, i.e. your right to be you and live your life the way you choose, include all of the following:

"Assertive Rights

1) You have the right to judge your own behavior, thoughts, and emotions, and to take the responsibility for their initiation and consequences upon yourself.
2) You have the right to offer no reasons or excuses to justify your behavior.
3) You have the right to judge whether you are responsible for finding solutions to other people's problems.
4) You have the right to change your mind.

54

5) You have the right to make mistakes – and be responsible for them.
6) You have the right to say, "I don't know."
7) You have the right to be independent of the goodwill of others before coping with them.
8) You have the right to be illogical in making decisions.
9) You have the right to say, "I don't understand."
10) You have the right to say, "I don't care."
    You have the right to say no, without feeling guilty."
    By Manuel J. Smith

Once you start to understand these basic rights, the next challenge is how to actually integrate and apply this understanding when dealing with other people, especially those who are trying to persuade you, pressure you, or manipulate you into doing what they want you to do. Let's take a brief look at some of the things you can do.

The "sandwich technique"

A good, constructive assertiveness technique to start with is what I call the "sandwich technique". The "sandwich technique" is a positive, assertive and respectful way to respond to other people's requests and demands. When using this technique, you respond to other people's requests or demands with sentences or statements, which are made up of two different parts.

In the first part of the sentence, you acknowledge to the other person that you have heard what he or she said. This is always a good start because it is a respectful way of showing the other person that you were listening. In the second part of the sentence, you give your response and tell the person what you think or feel about the request or demand.

Here are some examples of how to use the sandwich technique:

- Thank you for thinking of me and I have other plans for the weekend.
- I understand this means a lot to you and I'm going to have to say no.
- I hear what you're saying and I feel differently about the matter.
- I really respect your opinion and the way I see it is...
- Your friendship means so much to me and I'm going to have to decline your kind offer.
- I understand what you're saying and this is not something for me.
- I really appreciate you thinking of me and I have other plans for Saturday night.
- Yes, I can relate to what you're saying and from my point of view, it looks to me like...
- Thank you for thinking of me, I really appreciate your concern, and no thanks.
- You could be right, and it's not for me.

This is a respectful way to deal with other people's requests or demands because you first acknowledge that you hear the other person, and that you understand what he or she is saying (and even appreciate their interest or concern). Then you come with your response, which may be saying no or setting limits.

Here are some examples of conversations using this technique:

Example one: You get invited to a party this weekend. You don't feel like going. Here's your conversation with the host.

Host: We're really counting on your coming to our party on Saturday.

Your response: Thank you so much for thinking of me and I can't make it that evening.

Host: But we're counting on your coming.

Your response: I really appreciate your thinking of me and I can't come that evening.

If the person keeps on, you just keep repeating what you said. Sooner or later the other person will give up.

Example two: You get a new job offer. Even though it is an attractive offer, you don't have a good feeling about it. In fact, you feel sure there is something better in store for you.

Your friend/your mother: I really think you should take that job, it's such a great opportunity for you.

Your response: Yes, it is and it's simply not for me.

Your friend/your mother: But can't you see what a great job opportunity this would be for you. It would be so good for your career.

Your response: Thanks for sharing how you feel about this with me and I'm not going to take this job.

If the person keeps on pushing you, just keep repeating what you said until the other person gives up. He or she will.

In situations like this, it's a good idea to remember the other person probably won't agree with you and doesn't have to. Being assertive is not about winning arguments, convincing other people, or being right. Being assertive is about setting limits and taking good care of yourself. It's not about winning and losing. So be willing to hear and acknowledge the other person's point of view ("You could be right"), and then clearly state your own position ("and it's not for me"). You don't have to be defensive or come up with more and more arguments or explanations. It is better to just state your case and then repeat yourself.

You are responsible for taking care of you and the other person is responsible for his or her feelings and opinions about the matter. Each person has a right to his/her feelings and opinions. So again, you don't have to justify yourself, offer explanations, or find excuses for your choices. (If you want to explain yourself, that's okay, but the point here is, you don't have to. You have a right to your point of view, so you don't have to justify your choices.) Just state your case and then repeat yourself.

Here are some more good ways to acknowledge the other person's point of view while maintaining your own rights and point of view:

- I understand you feel that way, and in my experience, I find that...
- You could be right, and I prefer to do it this way...
- I think I can understand your point of view and I would rather not...
- I really appreciate your input in this matter and I still...
- I appreciate your thinking of me and the answer is no.

Here are the main points to remember when using the "sandwich technique":

- Acknowledge that you hear the other person. (Recognize their good intentions.)
- Then deliver your response.
- Use the word "and" instead of "but" when connecting the two parts of the sentence because the word "and" is inclusive.
- Don't expect the other person to agree with you.
- Don't be afraid to repeat yourself, kindly but firmly.
- You are responsible for your feelings and decision.
- The other person is responsible for his/her feelings about the matter.

As I said above, learning to be assertive and set limits like this takes practice. It's not something we can learn in a day or two because most of us did not learn how to be assertive in our childhood. This is why it can be really helpful to rehearse these kinds of situations in your head before and after they occur, especially if you've been in situations where you did not respond assertively in a good way.

For example, after a conversation where you feel you did not respond in the good, assertive way, try going slowly through a situation in your head afterwards and visualize how you would like to tackle a situation like this the next time it comes up. The more you practice mentally and rehearse these conversations in your head, the more you will discover that you can actually do this when situations like this do arise. Another good way to practice is to do this with a friend if you can – it's kind of like "play acting"!

Asking for time

Here's another good tip for beginners. When you find yourself in a situation where someone catches you off guard with a request and you're not sure how to respond – ask for time to consider the matter. This can be a very good idea when you're unsure how to respond. In situations like this, you can say: "Thank you for asking. Let me think about it and I'll get back to you." Or, "I'll have to check my calendar. I'll get back to you tomorrow." When you are unsure, asking for time can help in two ways:

1) It gives you time to think about the person, event, situation, invitation, possibility – and figure out what feels best to you. You might also discover there's another option, which feels better to you which you can suggest instead.

2) If your answer is no and you are afraid of the other person's response, asking for time will give you a chance to practice an assertive response, especially if you are worried that the other person might try to press you into saying yes.

Now let's go back to the party example above and see how asking for time works in this situation. In this case, when you get invited to the party, you're not really sure how you feel about going yet.

Host: We're really counting on your coming to our party on Saturday.

Your response: I really appreciate your thinking of me; let me look at my calendar and I'll get back to you tomorrow.

Host: But we're counting on your coming.

Your response: I really appreciate your thinking of me and I'll get back to you tomorrow.

If the person keeps on, you just keep repeating what you said.

By postponing your answer in this way, you give yourself time to figure out how you really feel about going and then you can plan how to deal with the situation assertively when you call back and respond.

When people continue to make you "wrong"

Unfortunately, even when we learn to be assertive in a good way, some people will continue to judge our behavior or choices as "wrong" and start telling us how to live our lives. This demonstrates a basic lack of respect for our right to be who we are. If this is the case in one or more of your relationships – and especially if this happens repeatedly – it can be helpful to understand what healthy boundaries actually look like and then know how to set them. When we understand the principles behind healthy boundaries, then we can more realistically assess what we can do to improve a relationship like this – or if we should, in fact, remove ourselves from the relationship.

Healthy Model No. 9

Healthy Boundaries

Having healthy boundaries is an important part of being able to take good care of oneself in a world with so much diversity and billions of people. To understand and have healthy boundaries is vitally important if we want to achieve and experience healthy interactions with our families, partners, friends, neighbors, relatives and colleagues. So let's take a look at what having healthy boundaries looks like and actually means.

To have healthy boundaries is based on, and grows out of, an understanding that we are separate individuals. In other words, you are you and I am me. This basic observation is true both physically and mentally/emotionally. In short, you are in your body and I am in mine – so this is the physical part of the equation. And in addition to that, you also have your own thoughts, emotions and experience of life and I have my own thoughts, emotions and experience of life – which is the mental/emotional part of the equation. This is pretty obvious stuff, and when we can see this, we can also see that because we are separate individuals, there is a *natural boundary* between us. We can see that I live in my head and you live in yours – and that we each live in our own mental universe. This is important to notice and understand – and remember. There is no one common experience that is exactly the same for every human being that has ever lived. (For more about this mechanism, see the Basic Observations in Part 2.)

It is also important to notice that no matter how much we love another person or how close we are to another person – be it our partner, our child, our parent, our friend – we cannot get inside the other person and think, feel or experience life in the way that he or she does. This is just the way it is. Please be sure you understand this and are completely sure of this. But this does not mean we cannot share our thoughts, emotions and experiences with other people. Of course we can. But we cannot get inside of each other and "feel" what another person is feeling. For example, if I have a pain in my knee, I can tell you about it, you can watch me, you can see me limp or look pale – but you cannot "feel" how my knee feels. And the same goes for me. If you tell me you have a headache or a stomachache, I can listen to you and observe you, but I cannot "feel" how it feels for you to have a headache or stomachache.

When we see and understand this, we can also see there is this *natural boundary* between us which I am talking about. It is the place where you "end" and I "begin". The place where your experience is being experienced by you and the place where my experience is being experienced by me.

Your territory and my territory

If we try to visualize this, we could say it's like you have your little plot of land – your territory – and I have mine. It's like you have your little garden plot where you have your little cottage – and I have my little garden plot where I have my little cottage. And it's your job to take care of your cottage and tend your little garden and it's my job to take care of my cottage and my little plot of land. So we each have our own territory – and then there is the place where our little gardens meet. And there, where our little gardens meet, that is where the natural boundary between us is. This is where your territory ends and where my territory begins. Or vice versa. My territory ends here and your territory begins there. That's just the way it is.

So let's visualize this boundary between our gardens as a little white picket fence. Now, if we have healthy boundaries, we respect this natural boundary between us. We respect the reality that you are you and I am me – and we act accordingly. So here is an example of what I mean and how this natural boundary plays out in action. Let's say I wake up one morning and the sun is shining and it's a gorgeous day and I look out my window and I can see you are over there in your little garden next door. And I think I really want to play with you! So if I have healthy boundaries, I go over to the little white picket fence between our gardens and knock and say, "Hi neighbor, do you want to play with me today?" And then you can answer. You can say, "Yes, I'd love to play with you, please come in," and then you open the little gate and invite me in to your garden. Or you can say, "No I don't want to play with you, today." Or you can say, "I have other plans for today." Or... there are so many things you can say. And if I have healthy boundaries, I respect your answer. It's as simple as that.

Lack of healthy boundaries

Unfortunately, the problem is many people don't have healthy boundaries – not in their families or in their relationships or at work or with their friends. So how does this look? What happens then? To illustrate this, let's take the same example and see what happens if I don't have healthy boundaries. It starts out in the same way. I wake up in the morning and the sun is shining and it's a gorgeous day and I see you over in your garden and I really want to play with you. So I jump out of bed, get dressed and run over to the little white picket fence. But this time, instead of knocking politely on the gate and asking you if you want to play with me, I go charging into your garden and grab you by the arm and say, "Now you're going to play with me! Let's have some fun!" This is a boundary violation because I didn't ask your permission first. I didn't ask you if you wanted to play with me, I didn't respect you or the fact that you might have other feelings or plans. I just forced myself into your space without asking. This behavior shows that I do not have healthy boundaries. I was disrespectful and violated your boundary, in other words, I did not respect your right to be you and make your own decisions.

But there's another aspect to this situation too – and that's you. If you are on the receiving end of such behavior (a boundary violation like this) and you are not able to take care of yourself and be assertive by saying, "Ho, stop right this minute. I didn't invite you in or give you permission to come barging into my garden and I don't want to play with you today," then you don't have healthy boundaries either. In other words, you were not assertive and able to take care of yourself, and have actually allowed another person to violate your territory and boundaries.

So here we can see that there are, in fact, two ways in which the lack of healthy boundaries manifests. The first is when a person doesn't simply ask for what he or she wants but just violates another person's boundaries. And the second is when a person's boundaries are violated and this person is unable to take care of or defend him/herself in a firm and assertive way and set a healthy boundary. In both cases, there is a lack of healthy boundaries.

So what can we do about this?

First of all just understanding the basic principles and Healthy Models for Relationships outlined in this book will go a long way to clearing up the misunderstandings that lie behind boundary violations. When we understand that we are all different and we are all having different experiences even in the same exact situation, it's much easier to behave respectfully and not take disagreement so personally.

Second of all, the more we understand the mechanism and can identify when boundary violations actually do arise, the easier it becomes to navigate respectfully and be assertive in all our interactions with other people – whether is it with our partner, family and friends, or at the workplace.

Identifying common boundary violations

Unfortunately, we are often at a loss when it comes to identifying boundary violations because we cannot figure out what actually happened. All we know is that we were in a situation with someone and we felt discomfort. Something didn't feel right, but because we didn't quite understand what actually happened, we were unable to analyze the situation.

Therefore, to help you see and identify boundary violations in a more concrete way here are some of the most common boundary violations. For each of the boundary violations listed below, you can be the one who violates another person's boundaries or someone else can be violating your boundaries.

Common boundary violations

Giving someone advice when the person didn't ask for your opinion

Good questions to ask yourself are:

- Do I give other people advice without them asking me for it?
- Is someone else giving me advice without me asking for it?

Telling another person how they "should" think or feel or live their life (when the person didn't ask for your opinion)

Good questions to ask yourself are:

- Do I tell other people how they should think, feel or live their lives when they didn't ask me for my advice?
- Is someone else telling me how to think, feel or live my life when I didn't ask for their advice or opinion?

Judging another person's lifestyle and making him or her "wrong" or "weird" or "strange" because he/she is different from you

Good questions to ask yourself are:

- Am I making someone "wrong" because he/she is different from me?
- Is someone else making me "wrong" because I do things differently than they do?

Telling another person you know better than he/she does, what or how the person is actually thinking or feeling

Good questions to ask yourself are:

- Do I have a tendency to tell other people that I know better than they do, what or how they are thinking or feeling?
- Is someone else telling me that he/she knows better than I do what or how I am thinking and feeling?

Making another person responsible for how you feel or for what you are saying and doing

Good questions to ask yourself are:

- Am I blaming someone or making someone else responsible for how I feel or for what I am saying and doing?
- Is someone else blaming me or making me responsible for their feelings or for what they are saying or doing?

Touching another person's body without their permission

Good questions to ask yourself are:

- Do I touch other people without their permission?

- Do other people (or someone specific) touch me without my permission?

Going through another person's personal possessions (like their phone or computer or bag) without their permission
Good questions to ask yourself are:

- Do I go through someone else's personal possessions without their permission?
- Is someone I know going through my personal possessions without my permission?

Any kind of aggressive or threatening behavior
Good questions to ask yourself are:

- Do I sometimes shout or threaten other people – even mildly? Do I sometimes, for example, wave my arms aggressively or kick or throw things?
- Is there someone in my life who shouts or threatens me – even mildly? Is there someone in my life who, for example, waves his or her arms aggressively or kicks or throws things?

This kind of behavior is completely unacceptable.

Any kind of violent behavior
Good questions to ask yourself are:

- Do I sometimes act violently towards others?
- Is there someone in my life who is violent towards me?

In cases like this, it is important to remember that we live in societies where there are laws to protect each of us from violence and abuse, and that this type of behavior is completely unacceptable. If you encounter this kind of a situation, leave as quickly as possible or call the police or your neighbors if you need help.

Each of the above boundary violations shows a lack of respect for the rights of each individual to live their life as he or she chooses. In addition, each of these boundary violations also indicates a basic lack of respect for the intelligence of other people and their ability to cope with and manage their own lives. When we understand the difference between boundary violations and having healthy boundaries, we can also more realistically assess what we can do to improve a relationship where there is a lack of healthy boundaries – or if we should, in fact, remove ourselves from the relationship.

Minding your own business

When we understand what constitutes boundary violations, we can then understand why a good general rule is to *Mind Your Own Business!* This means that unless someone asks for your opinion or advice or invites you into their space or life situation, stay in your own space. And mind your own business! This is a good general rule, but of course there are some important exceptions to this rule.

In brief, you are not supposed to mind your own business when you and another person have a shared project (like a home or children or a work project). Then you are both involved and you have just as much right to your ideas and opinions as the other person. When we have shared projects, it's more a question of how to communicate respectfully and reach workable compromises if we disagree as to how to deal with whatever the matter is (again, for example, the house, the children, the family vacation, the project at work, etc.). (See Healthy Model No. 5: *It's Not What You Say – But How You Say It* for some examples of the difference between respectful and disrespectful communications.) There are a few other very important exceptions to *Minding Your Own Business*. The first is obvious – that it's the job of parents of small children to take care of them and mind their business! But as children grow up and begin to take more and more charge of themselves and their lives, it is the job of the wise parent to back off and trust in the intelligence of their children. (For more about this see Healthy Model No. 14: *Sane, Realistic Parenting.*)

The second is when we go to a therapist or doctor or expert of some kind and specifically ask for (and often pay for) this person's advice.

The third is when we are witness to abuse or violence of any kind. Then it's our job, our business, our responsibility to step in and stand up for the victims, whether it's a child or a woman being abused in a relationship or any other kind of abuse. When we do not interfere and stand up for respect and justice for all human beings, we are actually enabling the abuse to take place and are, in fact, also a guilty party in the situation.

The bottom line

Respect is the bottom line when it comes to all our interactions with our fellow human beings. When someone treats you disrespectfully over and over again and is not amenable to your efforts to establish a respectful and constructive way of speaking and interacting, then the only thing left to do is walk away. The basic principle here is you have a right to be you. And that your right to be you and to be treated with respect (also when people disagree with you) is not up for negotiation.

Principle versus Content

Principle
- Every person has the right to be who he or she is
- This is the principle
- This principle is the basis of democracy

Content
- There are many different ways people can be
- There are many different ways people can think, feel and act
- There are many opinions about how people should be
- There are endless possibilities
- All this is content

Principle
Principle is your right to be you, regardless of anyone's opinion.

Principle is the right of other people to be who they are, regardless of anyone's opinion.

Democracies are law-based societies – designed to protect the rights of the individual – based on principle.

Freedom of speech, freedom of assembly, freedom of religion are the natural expression and consequence of these basic rights.

In democracies, there is room for diversity.

Democracies are non-judgmental.

All of the above is based on principle.

Principle versus content
When we apply this understanding of principle, we can see, for example:

Principle is:

- Every conversation should be respectful
- Each person has a right to his say and ideas

Content includes:

- Each person's ideas, opinions, etc.
- Endless possibilities
- People may disagree about almost all specifics (content)

More Good Constructive Communications Techniques

Here are some more good communications techniques which can strengthen our ability to be assertive, have healthy boundaries and communicate clearly, constructively and respectfully with our partners, families, friends and colleagues.

Negative inquiry – asking for more information

Negative inquiry is a great technique for stimulating clearer, more constructive communication between two people. And it also strengthens our ability to be more assertive in a respectful way.

Negative inquiry basically means asking for more information about what someone is saying, instead of just accepting everything a person says at face value. If you listen carefully to most people's conversations, you will discover that many of us aren't that good at communicating. Moreover, many people have a tendency to say things without really thinking them through (unfortunately). As a result, conversations may be filled with platitudes, assumptions, and generalizations. Furthermore, some people have a tendency to conflate or mix and link things together which don't really have anything to do with each other. As a result, you as a listener may find it difficult to understand what the person is actually saying, which can make it difficult to respond clearly and constructively.

Listening is important too

This is where listening comes into the picture. Learning to really listen to what other people are saying (literally), instead of just accepting unequivocally what someone else says, is an important part of learning to have healthy boundaries and be assertive. When you listen carefully to what someone says, you will be better able to identify when and where it is a good time to ask for more information or ask questions.

It's also important to listen to avoid the danger of coming to too hasty conclusions about what another person means. We might think that we know what the other person is talking about or means – without actually having checked if we understood them correctly. Which can even further confuse communications. So again, asking questions or asking for more information can help further clear, constructive communications between people. In addition, when we ask questions, this usually slows the conversation down a bit which is a good thing because it makes everyone stop and listen a little more carefully. Plus we are encouraging the other person to stop and think about what they are saying and actually explain what they mean.

Asking when you are being criticized

Asking for more information or asking questions is also a very helpful technique when someone is criticizing you or trying to persuade you or bamboozle you into doing something you don't want to do. Then it's usually a good idea to ask questions or to ask for a further clarification as to what the person means or really wants, instead of just immediately getting upset or defensive. It also helps uncover why this matter is so important to the other person – someone you might not necessarily know or understand. When you know why something is important to another person, you might better be able to come up with a constructive alternative solution or proposal.

So let's look at how asking for more information looks in conversations.

Tackling generalizations and platitudes

In situations where someone is generalizing or speaking in

clichés or platitudes, you can say, for example:

- I'm sorry, but I don't understand what you are saying. Could you be a little more specific?
- I don't understand, what do you mean by that?
- I don't understand, what's wrong with that?
- I really don't understand what you are saying – can you give me a concrete example of what you are talking about?

And when the person replies, if you still are unclear about what he or she is saying or means, you can again ask for more information and say:

- I still don't understand, why is that a problem?
- I hear what you are saying and I still don't understand what you mean. Can you give me a concrete example of what you are talking about?

Here are two examples of questioning platitudes:

Example 1: You are talking to your friend about how your mother wants you to join the family for the weekend and you really don't want to go.
    Friend says: ... that's just the way mothers are.
    You: ... just the way mothers are? I don't understand. What do you mean by that?
    Friend: Oh come on now, you know what I mean...
    You: No, I'm not really following you...
    Friend: All mothers are like that – how can you be so dense?
    You: All mothers are like what?
    Or you could ask: How am I being dense by asking you what you mean?

Example 2: You have a backache and are talking about it with your friend.

Friend says: That's just what happens when you get old.

You: I don't understand, what do you mean by that?

Friend: Oh come on, you know what I mean.

You: No I don't. What does having a backache have to do with getting old?

Friend: Well that's just what happens when you get old, you know that.

You: No I really don't. I don't see the connection.

Friend: Don't be silly now… everybody knows that the body just falls apart when you get older.

You: Really? I know lots of older people who are strong and healthy. And besides, what does getting old have to do with me? I'm only 42, is that what you mean by getting old?

Tackling criticism

Here is an example of questioning someone who is criticizing you:

Example 3: You are studying to get a bachelor's degree in "Gender and Sexuality Studies". Your father thinks your chosen field of study at University is rather "strange" and a waste of time.

Dad says: Why study "Gender and Sexuality"… of all the things?

You: I don't understand – what's wrong with studying "Gender and Sexuality"?

Dad: I just think it's a bit of a waste of time.

You: I don't understand – why is it a waste of time?

Dad: Because what kind of a job will you be able to get with a degree like that?

You: What do you mean?

Dad: Why not study medicine or become a schoolteacher? Something practical and in demand?

You: I still don't understand. What's wrong with having a degree in a new area where there might not be that many jobs available yet?

Dad: Well what's the point of getting a degree if you can't get a good job with it?

You: I'm not studying "Gender and Sexuality" just so I can get a job, Dad. I'm studying this because I'm passionate about the history of women, feminism, sexuality and other gender-based issues. So much is going on in the world today in these areas. It's so exciting!

Dad: Okay, okay... but don't you come asking me for money when you find out there aren't that many well-paying jobs out there for people with degrees in "Gender and Sexuality"!

You: Have I ever asked you for money, Dad?

Dad: I gave you money for the down payment on your car last year, didn't I?

You: Yes, you did, but did I ask you to give me the money?

Dad: No... you didn't.

You: As far as I remember, you gave me the money because you wanted to...

Dad: Yes, that's true, I did. I just wanted to help you – that's all. (Dad is silent for a moment) and then he says: And I just want to help you now too... I'm just worried about your future, that's all.

The conversation could end there, or you could say: I know you mean well, Dad, but when you talk disrespectfully about what I'm doing with my life, it doesn't further a good relationship between us.

Dad: I didn't mean it like that.

You: Well what did you mean?

Dad: Okay, I'm sorry. I'm just worried about your future – that's all.

You: Thank you.

Tackling criticism from non-assertive people

Negative inquiry or asking for more information can also be helpful in situations where the person you are interacting with is not particularly good at being assertive and respectfully asking for what he or she wants. So instead of asking straight out, the non-assertive person might try to persuade you or bamboozle you into doing something you don't want to do by criticizing you or your behavior in some way. In cases like this, it can really help to ask questions or ask for a further clarification as to what the person is really trying to say – instead of just getting upset or defensive. The good part about this tactic is that once you have (hopefully) stimulated the other person to state more clearly what he or she really wants or what he or she is upset about, then you can then deal with the situation more constructively.

Here is an example of how to uncover what another person really wants:

Example 4: Your partner doesn't like the fact that you're going to town with your friends on Friday evening. In a case like this, negative inquiry can help reveal what's really bothering your partner.

Partner: What's wrong with you? You're always going out partying with your friends.

You: I don't understand, what's wrong with me going out with my friends?

Partner: It's just too much. This is the third time this month you are going out.

You: Yes it's true this is the third time, but what's wrong with that? There have just been so many events to celebrate suddenly.

Partner: Because you're always so tired the next day.

You: Yes, sometimes I am. But why is that a problem?

Partner: Because then you're not fun to be with.

You: Why am I no fun to be with?

Partner: Because I want to do stuff with you too, dummy!

You: I'm glad to hear that, sweetheart. What would you like to do with me (big smile).

Partner: Oh, I don't know, nothing specific... but you are always so busy. You've got so many things going on all the time with meetings after work and going to fitness. And when you do have some free time, you're going out with your buddies... but what about me? Don't you care about me anymore?

Pause in conversation...

You: Yeah, I can see what you mean. We haven't been spending much time together lately. But I was also under the impression that you were really busy too with going to yoga and meeting your girlfriends...

Partner: But I'm not as busy as you are...

You: Okay, well tell me what you'd like us to do together...

Partner: I just want to spend some more quality time with you, that's all.

You: Okay, sweetheart, I'm sorry. I didn't know you were feeling like this.

Tackling boundary violations

Here is an example of how to tackle a boundary violation:

Example 5: Your partner threw out your old T-shirts without asking your permission.

You: Where are my old T-shirts?

Partner: I threw them out.

You: What?

Partner: They were so old and worn out, I just thought it was time to get rid of them and buy some new ones. Some of them even had holes in them!

You: I know they were old, but why did you throw them out without asking me first?

Partner: Like I said, I just thought it was time you got some new T-shirts.

You: Thanks for your concern, but they are my T-shirts. So why didn't you ask me first?

Partner: Do you really want to have all those old, worn T-shirts filling up your drawers?

You: I don't know, and you still didn't answer my question. Why didn't you ask me first?

Partner: I don't know… why are you getting so touchy all of a sudden?

You: I'm not getting touchy, I'm just asking you why you threw out my T-shirts without asking my permission first.

Partner: Oh, come on… you look so much better in new T-shirts…

You: You could be right… and when you throw out my T-shirts without asking my permission you are not respecting me and my things. So in the future, please ask me first before you throw out something of mine.

Partner: Okay, okay.

You: Thank you.

In conclusion, as we can see from the above examples, asking for more information can be a good way of stimulating clearer, more respectful communications between people, whether we are talking about dealing with vague, abstract generalizations and platitudes or prompting the other person to be more clear and assertive in telling you what is really bothering them or what they really want.

Stick to the point and stay on message

Another thing that can sabotage our ability to have constructive conversations with other people is that so many of us find it difficult to stick to the point and stay on message. Instead we might:

- Bring in or bring up past issues or disagreements
- Get personal and come with critical or derogatory remarks about the person in general
- Predict the future and threaten dire consequences if the person disagrees with us
- Compare this situation to other situations or to other people
- Refer to what other people say about something like this or use another person's opinion to justify our own
- Refer to some "arbitrary standard" such as "that's just the way we do things in our family" to justify our point of view
- Bring in other areas of the relationship where there are problems
- Cast doubt on the other person's good intentions or motivation and/or try to discredit the person

Unfortunately, by doing things like this we can quickly turn a relatively harmless discussion or disagreement into a major, emotional battle. So a discussion about who is going to do the dishes tonight can turn into big deal if you or the other person also bring up whose job it was to vacuum clean the house last Christmas or who was supposed to shop for... but forgot... or that time one of you forgot to pick up little Joey at kindergarten... yes the list of things that can muddy the water goes on and on.

This is why it's so important to try to keep the focus on the matter at hand. If someone brings up issues that have nothing to do with what you are discussing, you can politely remind the person you are talking to by saying, "Let's just stick to the matter at hand and wait with talking about who's going to drive little Joey to that party tomorrow." Or you can say something general like: "If you have other grievances or things you want to discuss, I'd be happy to talk about them some other time, but let's just deal with this matter first."

Staying on message is especially important in close personal relationships where we have a long history together.

Asking for a "Time Out"

Another valuable tool when it comes to navigating wisely in our conversations with other people is the "Time Out" technique. This is especially good when people get very emotional or if one or more of the people involved have a tendency to get angry very quickly and easily.

If this is the case and if things seem to be getting out of hand, it can be a good idea to call for a "time out" so everyone has a chance to cool off a little. When coaching couples, I often suggest that they talk about and agree upon this "time out" principle in advance when things are peaceful between them. Then if they find themselves having a heated discussion or argument about something – and one of the partners calls for a "time out" – then both parties will know what the other person is talking about because it's something they have agreed upon in advance.

Then when one person calls for a "time out", the two parties immediately stop their discussion or argument and simply walk away from each other. One person can go for a walk, or they can go into separate rooms... and take a cooling off period of at least 15 minutes (preferably longer) before they get back together and continue talking. Hopefully this will give each of the parties a chance to calm down, reconsider their strategy, and remind themselves how to communicate respectfully and constructively.

Dealing with sarcasm and uncovering inferred passive-aggressive statements and behavior

The negative inquiry/asking for more information technique that I describe in the beginning of this chapter is also a good tool when it comes to dealing with general, vague, hinted, inferred passive-aggressive attempts to criticize you or manipulate you.

Below is an example of how asking questions (negative inquiry) can help you deal with criticism which is delivered under the guise of humor and/or sarcasm.

In this connection, it is important to understand that non-assertive people often deliver criticism under the guise of sarcasm basically because they have not yet learned to speak up directly. By questioning their non-assertive tactics, we can (hopefully) encourage people like this to speak up and share their concerns and issues in a respectful manner.

Here is an example of how to use negative inquiry in a situation like this:

Jack and Jeanette are having dinner with friends. Everyone's having a good time until suddenly Jeanette starts entertaining the group by telling them about Jack and his two previous long-distance relationships. While she's talking and making fun of Jack, Jack feels hot and uncomfortable but doesn't really know what to do about it. People are laughing and Jack knows it's supposed to be funny, but it doesn't feel that way.

So what could Jack do? Should he just laugh along with the rest of the people or is there a constructive way to deal with a situation like this? Fortunately, there are good ways to tackle situations like this and negative inquiry is one of them. Instead of laughing along with everyone else, if Jack is relaxed enough about being himself and not being a perfect human being, Jack could ask Jeanette for more information about her story while she is talking. And if he isn't relaxed and brave enough to do this at the dinner table, he could at least ask her for more information when they get home later that evening.

Example 6: Jeanette makes fun of Jack at a party.

Here's what Jack could say at the dinner table (or later that evening when the two are home alone):

Jack: I don't understand, Jeanette, what's so funny about

having long-distance relationships?

Jeanette: Oh, come on, Jack, isn't it true that you've had TWO long-distance relationships!

Jack: Yes I have, but what's funny about that?

Jeanette: We both know how difficult it is for you to commit.

Jack: Now I'm really confused. I don't understand – what does having a long-distance relationship have to do with commitment?

Jeanette: Oops! You are really touchy about this, aren't you?

Jack: I still don't understand what you're saying. What do my previous long-distance relationships have to do with commitment?

Jeanette: Do we really have to talk about this now?

Jack: You're the one who brought all this up. All I'm trying to do is understand what you're talking about.

Jeanette: Sometimes I just don't know where I have you.

Jack: Could you be a little more specific?

Jeanette: Oh, come on. Can't we talk about this some other time?

Jack: Yes, of course we can. And next time you want to have a serious talk with me about commitment, please just say so – instead of making fun of me in front of our friends.

Jeanette: Okay, I'm sorry.

Jack: Thanks.

As we can see from the above, Jeanette is obviously feeling insecure and dissatisfied with certain things in their relationship. But because she is not good at communicating clearly and constructively, her concerns come out in a sarcastic, disrespectful manner. This is a classic example of passive-aggressive behavior. Because she doesn't know how to respectfully say things straight out, she covers up her wants and needs and makes fun of Jack instead. Something which, unfortunately, only makes things worse. The good news here is that when Jack asks for more information, instead of being defensive, he is taking the initiative and trying to start a constructive conversation with Jeanette about what's bothering her. Hopefully this will encourage Jeanette to speak up and honestly share her true thoughts and feelings so they can have a respectful discussion about how to deal with these issues and improve their relationship.

Respect

All the techniques presented in this chapter are designed to facilitate clearer, more respectful communications between people. As you have discovered, there are many chapters in this book, such as Healthy Model No. 2 about the levels of conversation and Healthy Model No. 5 about the way we say things, which address the challenge of learning and practicing respectful communications. But regardless of the situation or approach, respect is the bottom line when it comes to our interactions with our fellow human beings. How can we navigate wisely and respectfully with our fellow men and women based on the reality that we are all different and that each one of us has a right to be here and to be treated with respect, even when we disagree. Or should I say, especially when we disagree. This is the goal and our highest aim if we want to experience more peace and harmony in our interactions with our families, friends and communities.

Healthy Model No. 11

The Difference Between Anger and Personal Power

Many people perceive anger as a negative emotion. We often feel it's "wrong" to feel angry. So many people who are striving to be tolerant and loving and kind, suppress their own personal power because they mistakenly perceive the energy of personal power to be anger. Especially in situations where it would be more constructive to express their personal power by being assertive, firm and take good care of themselves by setting healthy boundaries.

But if we look closely at the energy most of us call "anger", we will see that what many of us call anger can actually be divided into two types of energy:

Aggressive energy

The first type of anger – which is what we call a "negative" or aggressive energy – is when we are disrespectful towards (or even attacking) another person. In cases like this we may be violating the person's boundaries or not respecting the person's right to be who he or she is with the choices and preferences he or she has. In other words, it is a disrespectful, aggressive, negative energy when we tell another person what to think, say, or do when this person hasn't asked for our advice and it's really none of our business (for more about the different kinds of boundary violations, see Healthy Model No. 9). This is a boundary violation, which is why it feels so uncomfortable to be on the receiving end of this type of energy. This aggression or anger is a negative energy.

Assertive energy

But there's another kind of energy which arises when someone violates our boundaries and this is what I would call "positive" or assertive anger or energy. You can also call this energy "healthy self-defense" even though energetically, it can "feel" like anger because it's a powerful, outgoing energy. But what is basically going on here is that when our boundaries have been violated, the natural impulse is to protect and defend oneself, which is a strong, healthy, positive energy. This energy is completely different from the energy that arises when we violate another person's boundaries.

When we slow things down and look carefully at the energy in this way, we can see that this powerful, out-going energy which we call "anger" can be either:

1)   *aggressive energy (violating someone else's boundaries)*
or
2)   *assertive energy or healthy self-defense (defending one's own boundaries and right to be who you are)*

Accordingly, we can see that healthy self-care involves being able to take care of oneself and protect and defend oneself from other people when our boundaries are violated or when someone does not respect our right to be who we are and choose how we want to live our lives. Exercising this prerogative is what personal power is all about. Personal power is the ability to be firm and assertive in a respectful manner (if possible) when necessary. Personal power is the ability to set limits and take care of oneself. Personal power is also the ability to protect oneself when someone else is aggressive (whether or not we do this in a respectful manner). Healthy self-defense and personal power are the ways in which healthy self-esteem/inherent worth manifests itself in the world. Which is why it is also called healthy self-love.

Consequently, when someone (or you yourself) tells you that you shouldn't be angry, please take the time to look closely at the situation and see whether what you are feeling is destructive, boundary-violating anger or healthy self-defense. When you can see what is really going on, you won't be in doubt. And then you won't give your personal power away.

In order to illustrate the difference between being assertive and being aggressive or passive, I've developed the chart below.

Passive behavior	Assertive behavior	Aggressive behavior
Flight	Balance Point	Fight
Running away	Your own power	Attacking
Submissive	Staying in your power	Dominating
Allowing others to violate your limits	Minding your own business	Violating the limits of others
Criticizing and blaming yourself	Taking responsibility for yourself	Criticizing and blaming others
Making yourself wrong	Standing up for your rights	Making others wrong
Pointing the finger at yourself	Personal power / Healthy self-defense	Pointing the finger at others

This chart shows that there is a balance point between the extremes of passive and aggressive behavior – and this balance point is assertive behavior. When you are assertive, you are staying in your own business and standing up for yourself and your rights. When you are passive, you run away from conflict and make yourself wrong. When you are aggressive, you attack and make other people wrong. The balanced position is assertive behavior – and means not going to extremes to deal with the situation but standing firm in your own power.

It's also interesting to notice that the passive types and the aggressive types seem to attract each other. Even though it is an unhealthy/dysfunctional relationship, the two are a good match (whether it's in a couple relationship or in a family or at the workplace). They are a good match because both believe the same story – that it is the passive one who is to blame or who is in the wrong. But once a formerly passive type learns to be assertive and stand firm in his or her personal power, then the aggressive type can no longer maintain his or her domination or control. Then typically the more aggressive person will either begin to treat the other person more respectfully or he or she will disappear from or leave the relationship.

When working with clients who have been non-assertive, passive people-pleasers, I often say to them that when they first begin to be more assertive, they can expect that the other person (the more dominating, aggressive type) will probably not take kindly to this change of behavior. This is because the previously non-assertive person is attempting to change the dynamic of the relationship. Which usually makes the dominating, aggressive type try even harder to maintain his or her domination and control. When this happens, if the previously non-assertive person stands his or her ground and continues to be more assertive then eventually the more aggressive person will either begin to treat the other person more respectfully or he or she will disappear from or leave the relationship. But it is realistic to expect that at first things may seem to get worse. I often say to clients – expect a few thunderstorms and other emotional explosions... but don't take them personally. It's just the other person testing you and trying to manipulate you back into your old non-assertive behavior.

Moving into personal power

There's another important aspect to consider when looking at owning our personal power. We discover this when we look at the levels of energy, which rise from negative to positive, shown on The Emotional Scale below. When we view things with this understanding, we can see that anger and then courage/personal power are crucial steps as a person develops in consciousness and moves upwards from the more negative levels of emotion to the more positive levels of emotion and consciousness.

In brief what happens is that the energy that we experience rises in power and positivity as we move from the lower, negative energy frequencies like shame, depression, fear, and anxiety into the higher, positive energy frequencies which begin with us taking responsibility for our lives and owning our power. Once we have owned our personal power, we can then move up the scale into willingness, acceptance and finally the ability to feel and experience real Love and appreciation in our daily lives. (For a more detailed explanation of the progression of energy frequencies shown here, see Healthy Model No. 13: *The Emotional Scale and the Levels of Energy*.)

The Emotional Scale

High, good-feeling energy

Love / Unconditional Love / Peace / Appreciation / Enthusiasm

↑

Mental / Rational thinking / Intellectual understanding

↑

Acceptance / Seeing life for what it truly is

↑

Willingness / Willing to participate in life and contribute

↑

Neutral / Allowing whatever happens to happen / non-attachment

↑

Courage / Personal Power / Taking responsibility for yourself

↑

Anger / Pride / Denial

↑

Fear / Anxiety

↑

Depression

↑

Guilt / Shame

↑

Low, bad-feeling energy

When we understand the Emotional Scale and this progression of energies, we can also understand that for many people, feeling angry is an important step in their evolution. Especially when it comes to feeling righteous anger and/or assertive energy when one has been treated disrespectfully or when one's boundaries have been violated. This is an important step because personal development is all about truth telling and taking control of one's own life. (See Healing Process No. 3: *Truth Telling.*)

The danger of "spiritual bypass"

In addition, when we understand the progression of energy frequencies and human evolution, we can also better understand that when we try to bypass important steps in our development, it usually doesn't work. (For more about the evolution of consciousness I highly recommend the works of David R. Hawkins such as his books *Transcending the Levels of Consciousness* and *Power vs. Force.*)

The progression of energies described in the chart above is the natural development of consciousness. Hence, when someone tries to jump from shame or fear to feeling unconditional Love (and forgiveness) for other people, it usually backfires because the leap in consciousness is too great. Which is why this type of behavior is often called "spiritual bypass". This leap in consciousness is just too much for an ordinary person to accomplish – to try and jump from shame, guilt and fear to unconditional Love and forgiveness all at once. It doesn't work like this because we have to grow and develop gradually up the Emotional Scale in order to integrate these changes and developments in our consciousness and lives. (Also see Healthy Model No. 13: *The Emotional Scale and the Levels of Energy.*)

I have seen over and over again in my many years of counseling and coaching people, that when someone who is a "doormat" and "people-pleaser" says he or she has forgiven the person or people who have been disrespectful towards them or violated their boundaries in the past – it's obvious that there is some kind of disconnect between this statement of theirs and their life situation. Because even though they say they have forgiven the other person, in reality, they are still on the receiving end of disrespectful or even abusive behavior. And why is this so? Because they have not yet learned to set healthy limits or assert their right to be here and to be treated with respect.

I often ask people like this the following questions:

- What about you? Don't you matter?
- Why are the feelings or ideas of these other people more important than yours?
- Don't you have a right to be treated with respect?
- How is allowing someone to treat you so disrespectfully being "loving and kind"?
- Wouldn't it be more loving and kind to yourself and to the other person to set healthy limits?
- How are you helping yourself or the other person if you don't have healthy boundaries and set limits and demand respectful behavior? What's "loving and kind" about this kind of behavior?
- Why are you afraid of owning your own personal power? (What are you afraid of?)
- What about you being loving and kind to yourself first? Why is this such a radical thought?
- Where did you learn that you don't matter? (Who taught you this?)

Then as we begin to explore these questions, people like this, sooner or later, discover there is simply no way around the basic mechanism – that one must own one's own personal power first. And that loving kindness has to begin at home with being loving and kind towards oneself. Which translates into having healthy boundaries and being able to take good care of oneself. This is what personal power is all about. Then, and only then, when you own your own personal power, is it truly possible to forgive and love others unconditionally.

So beware of trying to take too big leaps. Remember that being assertive, having healthy boundaries and taking good care of yourself is being loving and kind. Which is a vital step in your personal development and in the evolution of your consciousness. Vital steps that cannot be bypassed in the long run, no matter how much you want to be loving and kind towards others.

Many degrees of boundary violations

The reality is that boundary violations come in all shapes and sizes – from the mildest forms of boundary violations to the most dangerous and extreme forms of boundary violations. We can classify the degree or intensity of boundary-violating behavior as follows from:

Mild →
- Not so constructive behavior
- Not constructive, problematic behavior
- Disrespectful behavior
- Insulting, offensive behavior
- Aggressive, hostile, destructive, attacking behavior
- Abusive behavior
- Violent behavior
→ *Extreme*

In principle, a boundary violation is a boundary violation, whether it is mild or extreme. For example, whether someone gives you unasked for advice or steals your shoulder bag, money and mobile phone – both are boundary violations but the degree of intensity of the violation is obviously very different. And fortunately for most of us, nearly all the boundary violations we experience are at the mild end of the scale and arise because we (and our family and friends) are confused and ignorant about the importance of having healthy boundaries. And since most people mean well, talking to them about healthy boundaries and pointing things out to them is usually enough to rectify the situation and get the relationship back on track. (And even if this doesn't always happen immediately, most people will come to appreciate the value of healthy boundaries and constructive communications once they understand the importance of this for our relationships.)

But when we are assessing our relationships realistically it is also important to understand (and not be in denial about) the fact that the more extreme types of boundary violations do exist. And to understand that these types of boundary violations are serious violations of our human rights and can be dangerous to our health and well-being. Fortunately, most people never find themselves confronted with such extreme situations, but for those who do, it is so important to have a realistic assessment of who or what you are dealing with. And to understand that we have legal systems in democracies, which are designed to protect the legitimate rights of everyone, especially in the case of extreme boundary violations. In this connection, society does recognize that the behavior of psychopaths, sociopaths and other disturbed individuals or groups is not conducive or respectful, healthy behavior and must be stopped. So if you ever find yourself in such a situation, don't be afraid to ask for help immediately.

The Difference Between Essence and Form (Appearance)

Here is another Healthy Model for living that can help you gain clarity about your experiences and clear up much of the confusion about the situations you find yourself in. This model is based on the observation that there is (or can be) a difference between the outer or physical *form* (or appearance) of a relationship or circumstance and the way it "feels" to you (its *essence*).

Here's an example of what I mean by this. Let's take a relationship... two people who are married. On the surface, everything is the way it is "supposed" to be according to our social norms. We have a man and a woman, legally bound to each other, living in the same house, sharing the same space, having children together, and so forth. So from the outside, the "form" of this relationship is so-called "socially acceptable", "okay", "good", "proper", "normal". But if you know these people, if you get to hang out with them or be in their space, you may discover that it's quite a different story. There could be a lot of bad energy in the household, the partners could be fighting a great deal of the time, there could be a lot of tension or anger, shouting, or unhappiness, there could be a lack of respect, there could be boundary violations. In other words, even though the outer "form" of the relationship is in order according to our social norms, the "feeling" nature of the relationship is not good. It feels "off", "uncomfortable" or even "distressing". And this can be quite confusing to many of us. Especially when we are confronted with situations or relationships where the outer form is quite acceptable but we know in our hearts (often unconsciously) that the essence or the "feeling" of the relationship or situation is not. Hence, the information we are getting can confuse us. We feel at crosscurrents because there is a conflict between what our mind is telling us is okay and acceptable, and what our emotions are telling us about the way things "feel".

Gay or lesbian relationships are another type of relationship we can look at that can help us understand the difference between essence and form. Up until very recently, intimate relationships between two adult men, for example, were not socially acceptable and were even considered "criminal" offenses in many countries. (They still are even today in some countries.) But if we look at these relationships in terms of their essence instead of whether or not their form is socially acceptable, we can also see that often these relationships were good, respectful and loving relations between two adult human beings. In other words, these often were, and are, relationships where the essence feels good – regardless of whether or not the form is socially acceptable.

This is why it can be very helpful to understand in the various situations we meet in life that there is a difference between essence and form. It's a Healthy Model we can use to understand what we are experiencing. Moreover, it is important to understand that because we all have emotions and what I call an Inner Compass (see Healthy Model No. 7), each one of us is actually able to tell the difference between the outer form of something and how it actually feels. In fact, we can all do this. We can all tell the difference between what feels like love, kindness, good energy and respectful behavior, and what feels like tension, anger, frustration, irritation, bad energy and a lack of respect. This is just something we "know". Because we each have an Inner Compass and this is how we are wired. We can all "feel" the difference between good energy and bad energy, between comfort and discomfort. And we have always been able to do this – since birth. It's not something we have to learn.

But we often ignore this information or if we allow ourselves to "feel" it, we don't know what to do with the information our emotions are giving us because our feelings contradict our collective belief systems.

This conflict between what we feel and our collective belief systems can make family and couple relationships very confusing at times for many of us. Because on the surface, we may have what are socially accepted relationships according to our collective belief systems, but in reality, the essence or feeling of these relationships may be "off". In fact, the way some of these relationships are in reality may be way, way off. So even if the relationship or relationships have the accepted form or outer appearance, they don't "feel" good.

Some families, for example, don't live up to our collective myth that families and family members "should" be respectful and supportive of each other. Instead, behind closed doors, the reality is they treat each other horribly – as is the case in many dysfunctional families. And even if on the surface from the outside, everything appears "normal" and the family seems to stick together through thick and thin (another collective myth about families probably arising from our collective tribal background), there is a basic lack of respect for the rights of each individual family member. And again, when we come in close contact with these people and situations, this is what our feelings are letting us know – that in reality, things don't feel good. There is a basic lack of kindness and respect.

The mother-child relationship and the difference between essence and form (appearance)

Let's take another example: the common idea or belief that a child needs his mother. Most of us would nod our heads immediately and say yes, obviously! All children need their mothers. But if we look more closely at what we actually mean when we use the word "mother", we actually mean that all children need nurturing, love, warmth, care, support, understanding, comfort, and a sense of safety and security. That's what we actually mean when we say a child needs his/her mother because this is what we associate being a "mother" with.

But when we look at reality, unfortunately not all women who are mothers are able to provide their children with love, warmth, care, support, understanding, comfort, and a sense of safety and security. And usually, it's not because they don't want to, but rather because of their own issues, their life situation, background and/or programming. But because of this, some women are so challenged and confused that they actually are unable to provide for these most basic needs for warmth and nurturing in their child or children. And in some cases, these mothers can, in fact, be the source of the child's anxiety, discomfort, fear, insecurity. So in cases like this, we can be confused if we don't understand that there is a difference between essence and form. In a case like this, the form seems "right" because after all, this woman is the child's biological mother. But the essence tells us another story – the essence feels "off" because it feels really uncomfortable and sometimes downright unpleasant or abusive.

The relationship between siblings and the difference between essence and form (appearance)

Here's another example of what I'm talking about. A woman came to me for counseling and said she was so upset because she felt her sister didn't understand her and should be more supportive. When we delved into the matter, the woman wailed, "But she's my sister! My sister! She should support me and understand what I went through during the divorce. I'm just so furious at her for siding with my ex-husband and not being supportive of me and my children. How could she do that? How could she? We're family! I just can't understand her and I'm so disappointed."

Again, this is another good example of the difference between essence and form. This woman could not see that the reality of situation was very, very far from her ideas and expectations to family. The fact that her expectations didn't match reality – and were, in fact, very far from reality – caused her a great deal of pain and anguish indeed. (And remember, we're not talking about our preferences here. Because of course everyone would prefer to be loved and understood and supported by their family members. What we're talking about here is reality – the way things actually are.)

More examples of the difference between essence and form (appearance)

Here a few more examples of the difference between essence and form that I am sure you will recognize:

- Just because a person is successful (commercially, financially, popular, etc.) in their chosen profession (a businessperson, an artist, a sports person, etc.) – does that necessarily mean that their essence is healthy and feels good? Does that necessarily mean that the person is respectful, has healthy boundaries, and is kind and supportive?

- The opposite may also be true: Just because a person is not very successful financially or materially and is not very well-known or popular – does that mean that the person cannot be respectful and kind – and have a high level of consciousness? In fact, behind their humble exterior, the person might actually be a Buddha at the gas pump!

- Or what about politicians? We may or may not agree with their political views – but what about the way in which they conduct themselves? What about the way a politician communicates his or her views? Is this person respectful and constructive? Or is he or she disrespectful, destructive and polarizing?

- What about Gandhi? According to many of our modern-day standards as to what makes a person "successful", Gandhi was not very successful in terms of "form". Materially speaking, he was just a skinny Indian in a dhoti (a loincloth) who didn't own much more than the rice bowl he ate from. But what about his essence? What about his values, what about his unflinching dedication to the brotherhood and sisterhood of all human beings? What about him being the liberator of India?

- What about extraordinarily gifted artists like Van Gogh? At the time of his death he was not successful at all according to many of our modern standards of what constitutes success (form). He died penniless and alone at age 37... but does that mean that he was not a great visionary and artist (essence), regardless of the accepted views of society at the time and even today? Ironically today his paintings are some of the most coveted and expensive in the world, selling for over $100 million dollars each!

- What about beauty and fitness? Another area where we tend to focus almost exclusively on form. Is beauty and fitness a sign that the person is necessarily a kind and respectful human being? Someone with good energy? And just because a person is not so beautiful or fit, does that necessarily mean this person cannot be a kind, wise and wonderful human being? And what about ageism? As people get older and perhaps less fit, does that change their essence? Their level of maturity, wisdom and understanding?

The difference between essence and form (appearance) at the workplace

Relationships at work can also be highly problematic because of the difference between essence and form. Especially when a superior or boss is disrespectful. The problem is usually more difficult here because a workplace is not a democracy. An employee is hired to do a specific job and usually has a clear job description. Consequently, if you are an employee, there is usually a clear understanding in terms of what you, as an employee, are hired to do.

However, how a boss or superior goes about monitoring an employee's work performance can be respectful or disrespectful. And of course, we all have met or heard stories of bosses who have been disrespectful, unkind, unpleasant and/or downright abusive and boundary violating. Learning to be more assertive, take better care of yourself and having healthy boundaries can be a great help. But if these efforts don't improve the situation, then it will be up to you – as an employee – to decide how much your survival depends on staying at a particular workplace if you are not being treated respectfully. If you can leave and find work elsewhere, that is probably the best choice when all else fails in situations like this.

As to the relationship with colleagues, this is usually more amenable to working on communicating constructively and having healthy boundaries since you and your colleagues are equals (on the same level) – at the workplace.

But in either case, whether it is your relationship with your boss or with your colleagues, understanding the difference between essence and form will undoubtedly help you understand what you are experiencing and it will also help you to navigate more wisely at the workplace.

But to get back to the main focus of this book – families and close relationships...

The difference between essence and form (appearance) – going deeper

Now that we are a little clearer about the difference between essence and form in terms of our relationships, we can understand why it is so important to continue to investigate our basic beliefs and premises about our relationships and this thing called Life. Because when we innocently believe in flawed premises about relationships and Life, we end up having impossible and unrealistic expectations to many of our relationships. And we overlook the difference between essence and form, especially when it comes to our families or in our couple relationships. Which can make it so very confusing, painful and difficult for us to navigate wisely through these relationships and in our various life situations.

But the good news is that when we study and understand the Basic Observations and Healthy Models for Relationships outlined in this book, we can wake up from the trance of our collective myths and belief systems about families and relationships. And when we do this, we can also begin to understand that just because we are "family", it does not necessarily mean (or guarantee) that we can, or will, understand each other or that we can, or will, have anything in common. Just because we are family, it does not mean that people have the same thoughts, values or belief systems. Nor does it mean that people automatically treat each other with respect, just because they are "family". It just doesn't work like that.

If you are in doubt about this, please read the observations in Part 2 of this book – and then observe what is actually going on around you. Just watch how people think, talk and act until you can confirm for yourself that every human being is actually a distinct and separate individual – each with his or her own separate thoughts and beliefs, regardless of the family they belong to. This is why it is possible (and so often happens) that people in the same families have very different thoughts and beliefs about so many things. And because of that, often have very little – if anything – in common. That's just the way it is. Again, we're not talking about right or wrong here or how things "should" be – we're talking about what's really going on, we are talking about reality. We're talking about the setup here in this Life experience.

The myth of family

When we discover that many of our ideas about family and relationships have nothing to do with reality, we can better understand the discomfort we may experience when we are together with the people we call "family". We can better understand that even if the outer form is "correct", in other words, these people really are our "family", the essence is not because our feelings tell us that this relationship doesn't feel good.

Regardless of what our rational minds are saying, our feelings tell us that there is a lack of respectful behavior here because we feel a lot of discomfort. And as a result, there is a lot of bad energy. Which is where the mind often kicks in again and says, "But how can this be? These people are my family! They should understand and support me." But if you allow yourself to observe and feel, you will know that the heartfelt element is not there. It just doesn't feel like kindness or respect or love and support. There is no real warmth there. If this is the situation, the reality, and you allow yourself to feel your emotions, you will not be in doubt about what's going on. You will not be in doubt if the collective myth of the supportive family actually holds true for your family. Because you can ask yourself: Does the concept of a warm, loving, respectful supportive family match the reality of my family? And even if you wish the answer was yes, even if you wish it was the case, your heart and your Inner Compass will tell you the truth.

Just notice – and set yourself free

So what can you do about this? Well, first of all, wake up to the fact that there is a difference between essence and form. Just meditate on this idea for a while and then notice the difference between the essence and form in the various relationships you are involved in.

It can help to ask yourself questions like:

- Is there a feeling of respect here in this relationship?
- Is there a feeling of heartfelt warmth or is it just perfunctory?
- And if the feeling is just perfunctory (in other words, just obligatory) is there at least a feeling of basic politeness?
- Are the interactions in this relationship polite and respectful? (See Healthy Model No. 2 for a description of *The 3 Levels of Conversation* for more about this.)
- Am I respectful towards the other family members or the other people/person in this relationship?
- Do I respect (as the absolute minimum) the rights of other people to be who they are and to have their beliefs and lifestyles?
- Are the other people or family members respectful of me?
- Is there at least (as the absolute minimum) a basic respect for who I am and my right to be me?
- Do I have healthy boundaries?
- Do the other people have healthy boundaries?
- Can we talk about our differences in a polite and respectful manner?
- Can we be together respectfully without agreeing on everything?

Unfortunately, quite a few families pay lip service to the idea of democracy and everyone's right to exist and be who they really are – but in practice, it's quite another matter. Often people on the receiving end of intolerance and disrespectful behavior tolerate disrespect and even abuse from family members that they would never tolerate from friends or other people they meet out in society. But they do this in these situations because "it's family". But the reality is, our feelings are always letting us know.

The same holds true in some couple relationships, unfortunately. This is the most obvious in a sick relationship where we have an abusive man who say he "loves" the woman he is abusing. Talk about a lack of respect – talk about confusion. But again, there are also some women in situations like this who are so confused about what is going on that they can't see the reality of the abuse. And this is because the "form" of the relationship looks "normal" and because he says he "loves" her. But again, the reality of what's really going on and the way it feels are quite different.

So again, to free yourself from the collective belief systems about family and relationships requires waking up from these misunderstandings and the flawed premise that form and essence are the same. They are not – regardless of what anyone else tells you. Form and essence are two distinctly different aspects of any relationship. Notice this for yourself. Observe this for yourself. Notice how things feel. Understand that whether or not you are family, you have an Inner Compass and you have emotions which are signals from within which are, at all times, telling you how things feel. So listen to the signals from within and ask yourself the basic questions listed above. And remember, family can be highly overrated! While other types of relationships can be highly underrated.

Then notice instead where you actually do "feel" true kinship or friendship or understanding and support. Notice where the genuine good feelings really are. Sometimes it may be in relationships that society finds "strange" or "unacceptable". As mentioned above, this was obviously the case for many, many years – and still is – for gays, lesbians and transgender people around the world. But if this is reality, then what? What do we do? What can you do? My suggestion is – only you are inside you and only you know how things feel to you. Have confidence in that and take your power back – and then go after the essence of things – and forget about the form nature.

Healthy Model No. 13

The Emotional Scale and the Levels of Energy

When we look at the nature of this thing we call Life, i.e. the Nature of Reality, it is important to understand that there are different types or levels of energy. This is something we can all confirm for ourselves – and something that is important to understand if we want to better understand our Life experience and figure out how to navigate more wisely and happily through Life.

Now what do I mean by the different levels of energy? Everyone knows there is a difference between our various emotions and how they feel. We all know there is a difference between the way love, satisfaction and contentment feel, and the way anger, frustration and depression feel. Each one of us can "feel" the difference between these various emotions. This is no mystery because every emotion has a distinct feeling or energy. This is because each emotion or feeling is vibrating at a distinct or specific frequency. This means the way we can distinguish between the various emotions is by the way they "feel" or the frequency at which each emotion is vibrating. Consequently, we can (and do) categorize our emotions by the frequency (or feeling) each one has. And this feeling or frequency is the level at which this energy is vibrating. (For more about the scientific explanation of this phenomenon, I highly recommend the books of David R. Hawkins such as *Power vs. Force* and *Transcending the Levels of Consciousness*. Or the teachings of Abraham, through Esther and Jerry Hicks.)

Here is a chart which shows the Emotional Scale and the various levels of energy and how they feel:

High, good-feeling energy

↑

Love / Unconditional Love / Peace / Appreciation / Enthusiasm

↑

Mental / Rational thinking / Intellectual understanding

↑

Acceptance / Seeing Life for what it truly is

↑

Willingness / Willing to participate in life and contribute

↑

Neutral / Allowing whatever happens to happen / Non-attachment

↑

Courage / Personal Power / Taking responsibility for yourself

↑

Anger / Pride / Denial

↑

Fear / Anxiety

↑

Depression

↑

Guilt / Shame

↑

Low, bad-feeling energy

As we can see in the chart above, we can categorize the various levels of energy or emotions on a scale from high to low. The more good-feeling an emotion is, the more powerful the energy is and the higher the vibrational frequency of the emotion is. The less good-feeling an emotion is, the less powerful the energy is and the lower the vibrational frequency of the emotion is. This is why we can categorize the levels of energy as seen above. This is why I call this chart – the Emotional Scale.

It's also important to realize that the higher the level or

frequency on the Emotional Scale, the more in alignment we are with our True Selves and the Great Universal Intelligence. This is actually what our emotions and our Inner Compass are telling us. See Healthy Model No. 7 about the mechanism I call the Inner Compass. In brief, our emotions are telling us that the better we feel, the higher we are on the Emotional Scale in terms of how we regard Life, other people, and ourselves. And this means, the better we feel, the more in harmony we are with the Great Universal Intelligence that created all of us and this entire Universe.

To sum it up, the higher the level of energy or frequency of an emotion, the better it feels. In general, people who are higher on the Emotional Scale are happier in their daily lives. Their experience of life is happier and more satisfying than the experience of people who are lower on the Emotional Scale. In addition, because the energy of the higher frequency emotions is much more powerful than the energy of the lower frequency emotions, when we feel good and our energy is high, we not only feel better and more expansive, we are also more powerful. This means, interestingly enough, that our ability to help and influence other people in positive ways increases because we are more and more in alignment with the Great Universal Intelligence which is All-Powerful Infinite Energy. The opposite is also true: When we are experiencing the less good-feeling emotions, our energy is lower because we are out of alignment. Which means we don't enjoy life so much and our ability to be of benefit to ourselves, our families, and the world around us, decreases.

I suggest you take the time to notice the people around you during the course of your day. When you do, you will discover that, in fact, you already "know" and can identify the frequencies of the various people you encounter on your pathway through Life. In other words, you can identify where these people are on the Emotional Scale. We all know when we meet someone who is generally "angry" about lots of things and complains a lot or blames other people for their problems. It's a distinct "feeling" and vibrational frequency, so many of us avoid people who are complainers or who are angry all the time because the energy they are emitting just doesn't "feel" good. Many of us also know what it feels like to be around someone who is joyful, passionate and enthusiastic about Life and who loves Life and what they are doing. Many are instinctively drawn to people like this and like to hang out with them. This is just the way it is. Our ability to "sense" the vibrational frequency of other people just happens automatically, even though we might be unaware of why we move towards or away from certain people.

Our average frequency defines our placement on the Emotional Scale

When considering the Emotional Scale, it's also important to understand that when we characterize someone's frequency, we are talking about their average frequency or level of energy. Most people fluctuate back and forth through the various levels of emotion during the course of a day, but each one of us also has a certain "average" vibrational frequency or set point which characterizes who we are. This is why we can say someone is generally positive and optimistic, while someone else is generally grumpy or pessimistic. It's the average frequency we are talking about, which is also why we can identify the differences in the people we meet.

The other thing that is so important to understand here is that each one of us is emitting the frequency or energy of the emotions we are feeling. Each one of us is like a radio transmitter, sending out a signal to the Universe – a signal which is the level of our emotions or our average vibrational frequency. And because of the Law of Attraction, we attract back events, circumstances and people that match the frequency of the energy we are sending out into the Universe. This is why happy, positive people tend to attract more happy, positive situations, events and people into their lives, while grumpy, angry people tend to attract events and people which confirm their grumpiness and anger... Therefore, Life tends to be a self-fulfilling prophecy. Because what we focus our attention on is both the cause and effect of our vibrational frequency, and what we focus our attention on grows in our experience. Hence, we attract more of the same. (For more about the power of our focus, see my books *The Road to Power – Fast Food for the Soul* and *The Awakening Human Being – A Guide to the Power of Mind*.)

You can't take too big leaps

Another interesting aspect of this mechanism is that most of us cannot jump too far from where we are on the Emotional Scale. This means, for example, that people who are generally anxious and fearful can't jump to being loving and kind all the time even if they theoretically would like too. The distance from where they are at present on the Emotional Scale is just too great. This also means that someone who is often, or almost always, angry and complaining would have a hard time all of a sudden becoming accepting and allowing all the time. Again, the leap is just too great.

This mechanism is important for all of us to understand when we look at our own experience because so many people have unrealistic expectations to themselves (and to other people) when it comes to how they believe people "should" think and feel. That is why this Healthy Model includes the understanding that as we evolve and grow, we can only move to the next "better feeling" position on the Emotional Scale, relative to where we actually are at present. In most cases, this is the only movement that is possible, especially if we want to sustain our new position. But unfortunately, when someone tries to jump too far on the Emotional Scale, even if the person can get there and feel the energy momentarily, he or she will most likely discover that they cannot maintain the energy for long because the leap is too big. They cannot stabilize themselves there. It's just not possible or doable.

This also explains why a person who has been very sad, depressed or anxious is actually moving up the Emotional Scale and Levels of Energy (towards the better feeling energies) when he or she starts to feel angry. Being angry is the next level up the Emotional Scale from depression and fear and is a more powerful frequency than fear, anxiety or depression. So even though anger is still a so-called negative emotion, it is often the next necessary step for people in the process of reclaiming their personal power and moving into courage. This is especially true if the person has been very fearful and has been on the receiving end of boundary violations or any kind of psychological abuse. (For more about this mechanism, see Healthy Model No. 11: *The Difference Between Anger and Personal Power.*)

The Pyramid of Evolution

If we look at all of humanity in general, we will see that each and every person is evolving during their Life experiences and that some people actually move up the Emotional Scale during their lifetime. But many people do not. In fact, the vast majority of people remain more or less on the same level all of their life. According to David R. Hawkins, the world's leading researcher and expert in mapping out and calibrating the levels of consciousness, more than half of the world's population are vibrating on the lower levels of consciousness, i.e. on the levels below Courage. This means that a large part of the world's population is vibrating on average on frequencies where the energies are negative, in other words, the energies are not life-supportive or life-giving.

The Level of Courage marks the great shift in consciousness from negative energies to positive energies. This is because when a person reaches the level of Courage, that person goes from blaming other people and outside forces and circumstances for his or her experiences and problems – and begins to have the courage to take responsibility for what's going on in his/her life. Thus, we see that Courage is the level which signals a dramatic shift and transformation in a person's consciousness and vibrational frequency. From the level of Courage and upward, people are willing and able to look within and take responsibility and honestly ask – what is my part in this situation and what can I do about it? This is why all the energies from Courage upward are life-supportive and life-giving. In other words, they are positive frequencies.

As we move upward from the level of Courage, it is also interesting to note that there are fewer and fewer people the higher in consciousness we progress. Moreover, at the highest levels – the level of Unconditional Love and above – there are very few people. (Thus the pyramid of evolution, i.e. the higher in consciousness the fewer people there are.) There are very few people on Earth who are so highly developed and so high in consciousness as the truly great souls like the Dalai Lama or Mother Teresa. Fortunately for us, it is people like these few, whose frequency is so high, who have such an amazingly powerful influence for Good on the world and on all the people around them. For more interesting information about the evolution of consciousness, I highly recommend reading David R. Hawkins' books. The information he presents is truly eye-opening.

One of the great benefits of understanding the Emotional Scale and the levels of energy is that when we can see and identify where people are in their development, we can also be more realistic about who they are and what to expect from them. Moreover, we also understand that we cannot judge what's best for anyone else because it all depends on where this person or these people are in their evolution. This is also why there is no one right solution, no one perfect solution, which works for everyone. Because once again, it all depends on who you are and where you are on the Emotional Scale.

Healthy Model No. 14

Sane, Realistic Parenting

Most people sincerely want to be "good" parents, but what does sane, healthy parenting actually look like? How do sane, healthy parents actually talk and act – with other people and with their own children? Parents' behavior is one of the main things that children learn from and copy automatically and unconsciously, and carry over into their adult lives. When we understand this, we can see that our most important job as parents is to ourselves be kind, respectful human beings and to then teach (through our own words and actions) our children what respectful behavior looks like and translates into in our daily living. We do this also by explaining over and over again to our children, as simply and clearly as we can, what the basic principles and healthy models for relationships are. And by demonstrating this in practice by setting healthy guidelines for behavior in the home and in the world at large as our children begin to interact more and more with family, friends and other people outside the home.

These healthy guidelines for behavior can be divided into two categories:

1) The basic democratic principles and healthy models for respectful behavior outlined in this book
2) The practical ground rules (house rules) for living in a particular family

Let's look at these two categories.

The basic democratic principles and healthy models
In brief, it is the parents' job to teach our children the basic democratic principles and healthy models outlined in this book

which include the following basic rights:

- Everyone has the right to be who he or she is.
- Every person has the right to have his or her own thoughts, beliefs and feelings (because they do).
- Everyone should be treated with respect.
- This translates into having healthy boundaries and being assertive (see, for example, Healthy Models No. 8).
- Plus the ability to engage in constructive, respectful communications when dealing with other people (especially those with whom we disagree).
- In addition, it means teaching children the importance of being committed to work towards finding "workable compromises" whenever possible with their family and friends when there is disagreement.
- And finally, there must be clear consequences for children when they do not respect the rights of others and these basic principles. This means that when children are disrespectful, impolite and/or physically inappropriate (for example, pushing, shoving, throwing things, etc.) with their friends, siblings or other family members there must be consequences.
- See the charts on the following pages.

Unfortunately, because most of us so-called "adults" did not learn these basic principles and skills during our own childhood, it is difficult indeed for us to teach these basic principles to our own children. Thus, understanding and being able to identify healthy, respectful behavior in general is our first task if we want to be able to impart this knowledge to our children.

It is also important to understand and recognize that teaching these basic principles to our children is so much more important than any of the practical stuff we teach our children like playing games, being fit and sporty, cooking, cleaning, helping around the house, learning skills, and than even going to school to learn other skills. All of which are far less important than the basic people skills described above and throughout this book. Basic people skills are so important because the reality is that we human beings are inter-relational creatures. Meaning we are creatures who think, talk and have opinions and feelings about everything. Animals are also inter-relational, but they don't think and talk. And this is what distinguishes us as human beings. Thinking, talking and interrelating is how we share with each other and how we are in the world. So the real question is how can we talk and interact wisely and respectfully with our fellow human beings? Which is what good people skills are all about. And which is why it is the most important skill we can teach our children. (During my many years of coaching, clients have said to me over and over again – "Barbara, why didn't they teach us this in school??? If only I had learned all this when I was young!" And well, hopefully we will soon be teaching these basic principles to our children both in our homes and in our schools.)

The practical ground rules (house rules)
In addition to teaching our children the basic democratic principles and healthy models for respectful behavior, it is the parents' job to clearly determine and communicate to the children the practical ground rules for a home. But it is important to note that these ground rules will vary from home to home depending on the parents' preferences and mutual agreements. In addition, these basic ground rules will change and evolve as the children grow older. Examples of practical ground rules are: For small children, we wash our hands before dinner and brush our teeth before going to bed. We don't bring our iPads or smartphones to the dinner table. Lights out at 8pm, etc. Once again, obviously these rules or guidelines evolve as children grow older, but in all cases, there should be clear consequences for the children when the ground rules are not followed. Consequences can

include, for example, going to your room, no dessert tonight, a deduction from the child's allowance, less TV time etc.

BASIC DEMOCRATIC PRINCIPLES
RIGHTS AND RESPONSIBILITIES (CHILDREN)

Children's Rights	Children's Responsibilities
You have a right to be you.	You are to respect other people's right to be who they are.
You have a right to have all your thoughts and feelings.	You are to respect that other people have the right to have all their thoughts and feelings.
You have a right to have your opinions about everything.	You are to respect that other people have the right to have their opinions about everything.
You are to be treated with respect.	You are to treat other people with respect.
	You are to respect the ground rules in your family.

Ground rules (laid down by the parents)
(When raising children, it is the parents who decide
on the ground rules and on the consequences
for not following the ground rules.
This is not a democratic process
in which small children have a say.)

Consequences for children
(if the basic democratic principles above and the ground
rules are not respected)

BASIC DEMOCRATIC PRINCIPLES
RIGHTS AND RESPONSIBILITIES (ADULTS)

Rights	Responsibilities
You have a right to be you.	You are to respect other people's right to be who they are.
You have a right to have all your thoughts and feelings.	You are to respect that other people have the right to have all their thoughts and feelings.
You have a right to have your opinions about everything.	You are to respect that other people have the right to have their opinions about everything.
You are to be treated with respect.	You are to treat other people with respect.
	You are to respect the agreements you make with other people.

Agreements (between partners, in families concerning for example):
Healthy adult relationships are democracy in action.
Adults/parents/couples together make joint agreements
concerning joint activities, projects, the home, children, etc.

Other considerations
In addition to teaching our children respectful behavior and
healthy models for relationships, here are some other things to
keep in mind.

Everyone is unique

When we understand that everyone is unique and that we can't get inside another person and think or feel for them, then we can also understand that we can't "fix" or control or change another person – even if this person is our beloved child. That is the deal – that is the setup here – that is reality. And this holds true regardless of how well-meaning our intentions may be. Or how much we love another person, including our child or children, or how much we want to protect the other person (even our child) from discomfort or difficulties. We simply can't get inside other people and fix, control or change them and their experiences. It's just not possible. It's not up to us. But before I go any further, let me make it clear that I am not talking about not taking care of and protecting our children, especially when they are small. That, of course, is a parent's job. What I am talking about is trying to control (or believing that one can and should control) the internal experiences of our children (their thoughts and feelings). Unfortunately, this is where so much confusion arises when it comes to raising children.

So with this in mind – that reality is what it is and that we cannot get inside another person's head and control his or her thinking and feeling – how does this affect what sane, healthy and realistic parenting looks like?

Controlling a child's feelings

To begin with, let's look at what happens when parents try to control their children's feelings and experiences. And let's get real about this – most parents have tried, at some point in time, to control their children's feelings and experiences. Actually most parents have tried many times – countless times, if we are going to be honest. So ask yourself if you are a parent – haven't you tried to control your children's experiences? Probably... most probably. Because we all have good intentions and want our children to be happy. And we honestly believe that our children "should" be happy about the things we believe or want them to be happy about.

Most parents feel like this. But damn, have you noticed, reality is often different! So even if you really want your children to feel in a certain way, i.e. feel happy, they're just not with the program! Sometimes, no matter how hard we try, we just can't seem to make them happy when they're not. Yes, that's the reality. We believe they should know better or understand, but hey, they're still grumpy! So what do we do next? Many well-meaning parents will then try to soothe their children or explain to them or convince them or spoil them to get the emotional reaction they think their children "should" have. But heck, this almost never works – and if it does, well then it's usually only a short-lived fix. Which is why, sooner or later most of us discover that it's a hopeless project! Kids are how they are. Kids feel what they feel. Kids think what they think. It's just not up to us. And why? Because we can't get inside another person's head (not even our own dear, darling children) and control their thinking and feeling. This again is why we can't control their experience – no matter how hard we try.

So again, if you look closely, this also explains why you can be somewhere with your three children and you think this is a perfectly delightful experience, but one of your kids is still grumpy, and another one of your kids is happy and enjoying the situation, and the third seems lost in a dream. This tells us, again and again, that you can't control another person's experience because you can't get inside another person and think and feel for them. Period. That's just the way things are. That's the setup here. This is vitally important to understand if you want to live a happy life – and be a sane parent. The mechanism, the setup is what it is. When you understand the mechanism, then you can also begin to understand what you can actually do something about and what you can't do anything about.

But yes, as I said at the beginning of this chapter, it is your job as a parent to behave in the best possible way you can, and to be a respectful and loving parent and set healthy guidelines for living in your home. But once you've done that, it's a good idea to let the rest go because the reality is – no matter how hard you try – you can't get your children to think and feel the way you think they "should".

Moreover, if we look at situations like this very carefully, we will discover that it's also disrespectful on the part of parents not to trust in the intelligence of their own children. By this I mean, not to trust in the intelligence of our children and their ability to meet the challenges of life and learn from them and figure things out for themselves. But again, this doesn't mean we cannot set healthy guidelines for living and set limits in our homes for our children. But that's not the same as controlling how our children "feel" and experience Life. There's a very big difference here. So it's very important to be clear about this, because this is where the confusion arises.

The parents' job

Let's look closely at the parents' job. The parents' job is to provide a safe platform for their child or children to grow up and develop. Providing a safe platform includes teaching our children healthy models for respectful behavior as well as providing a safe home with food, clothing, education, health care, emotional support, and so forth. All of this is the parents' job and parents do this best by creating a home where there are clear, basic guidelines and ground rules, as to how we, human beings, can live together in peace and harmony while respecting each individual's right to be who he or she is. And this includes our children.

The basic democratic principles and ground rules in the home are pretty much like the rules of traffic. Red lights mean stop, green lights mean go. You drive on the right in this country (in some countries, you drive on the left). The speed limit is

… on the highway – and the speed limit is … in town. We all know about the rules of traffic and we all know that if we drive through a red light, or drive faster than the speed limit, we can get a ticket or be arrested. It's not a question of whether we like these traffic regulations or not, these are just the ground rules we humans have agreed upon and set up to facilitate the way people can live and move around together in the best possible way without crashing into each other. If you get stopped by the police because you were speeding, they don't ask you how this makes you feel or if you like the law. They're not interested in how you feel and don't care – all they know is you broke the law (the ground rules). And that has consequences.

The same goes for good parenting and the basic democratic principles and ground rules for peaceful living in a family. And this is where many parents get confused. Kids don't get a say in the basic democratic principles for respectful behavior or in making the basic ground rules – that's the parents' job. And kids don't have to like the basic principles or the ground rules – they just have to know they exist and understand that there are consequences if they do not treat other family members or other people with respect or if they do not follow the ground rules.

This has nothing to do with allowing, or not allowing, children to feel their emotions. And this has nothing to do with respecting the fact that every child is unique and that every child has an Inner Compass (for more about the Inner Compass see Healthy Model No. 7). Behaving disrespectfully or breaking the basic ground rules and experiencing the consequences is one thing. Feeling your emotions about what is going on is another thing. So when a child behaves disrespectfully or breaks a ground rule, it has consequences whether or not the child likes it. Parents are often confused about this and want their children to "like" or "feel good" about behaving respectfully and/or about following the ground rules and about the consequences of breaking the rules. But this is impossible. It's impossible to expect children to always "like" or "feel good" about following the basic principles and ground rules. And this is where parents today get confused. Children can dislike the basic democratic principles and the family's ground rules at times, and that's quite okay. The psychologically mature parent understands this, and is able to say, for example, "It's not respectful for you to throw things at your brother, I want you to stop right now" – and/or when it comes to the family's ground rules... "I know you don't feel like washing your hands before dinner, but that's the way we do things here in this house. When you're grown-up and have your own home, you can decide to do things differently, but as long as you live here, this is the way we do things in this house."

Parents are not respecting their children's right to be who they are and feel their feelings when they try to prevent their children from feeling what they are feeling. So it's important to distinguish between what respectful behavior is and what the ground rules are, and how children feel about following them. These are two different things.

For example, if a child dislikes a ground rule, that is his or her right and privilege as a human being because that's how the child feels. But this has nothing to do with following the ground rules. A child can dislike a ground rule all he or she wants, but the child has to follow it or there are consequences. It's as simple as that. Consequently, the clear message from the parent to the child should be: "This is the ground rule about this matter in this family, whether or not you like it and regardless of how you feel about it. If you break the ground rule, the consequences are..."

The confusion arises when the parent wants to control how the child feels about the ground rules and the various situations. Because then the message from the parent to the child is – *You shouldn't be "feeling" what you are feeling. You should feel the way I want you to feel. You should be happy and like something because I want you to.*

This is actually a boundary violation and disrespectful behavior from the parent's side because the parent is telling the child that he or she doesn't have the right to feel what they are feeling. The parent is basically telling the child what he or she "should" feel. This is disrespectful behavior from the parent's side. Healthy, respectful behavior from the parent's side says, "The ground rules in this house are that we wash our hands before dinner and we brush our teeth before we go to bed at night." The child can like this or not, but these are the rules – just like traffic regulations. And it's the parent's job to set up the guidelines and make the ground rules for the home – not the children's. A home where children are growing up is not a democracy in the sense that the children don't get to make the rules. It's the job of the mother and father to teach their children the basic democratic principles and to decide on the ground rules (house rules) for their home – but that's it!

More considerations

The above is not the same as saying that parents get to choose the child's pathway in life. In other words, it's not the parent's job to choose what subjects the child likes best in school, who the child likes to play with, what sports the child likes best, who the child wants to be friends with, what kind of books the child best likes to read, and how the child feels about a multitude of things and situations. Each child is unique and has an Inner Compass that is naturally guiding him or her in the direction of what feels best for them. And obviously, as children get older, the wise parents respect their children's intelligence and ability to make these choices for themselves. (The wise parent will try to explain to their children that everything has consequences, but that is not the same as trying to control a child's choices and preferences.) And as children mature and become teenagers and young adults, the wise parents will encourage them to find their own path, trust their own intelligence, and follow their Inner Compass when it comes to figuring out what's best for them and finding their pathway in life.

When we understand this mechanism, it leaves parents with the following. It's the parents' job to take responsibility for their own lives and their own happiness, and in this way teach their children (by their own example) what the setup here in this Life experience is. Clearly defining the basic democratic principles and ground rules in the home with clear guidance and clear explanations of the consequences of not following the rules will help children learn how to navigate in Life as wisely as possible. In addition, when children see their own parents living sane, responsible, and authentic lives, they will be more likely to follow their example. Again because the reality is that parents teach their children mostly by means of their actions and behavior (and not their words). The reality is that children naturally internalize the dynamic in their family of origin and unconsciously mimic various aspects of their parents' behavior because this is the model for life and for relationships they see and are exposed to. This is also why flawed belief systems and unhealthy behavior get passed down from generation to generation.

Things evolve and change

As children grow older, obviously things change and so do the ground rules (house rules). By the time children are teenagers or young adults, things have changed considerably. Young adults will have more freedom and greater responsibilities.

Two different parenting extremes

It is also interesting to notice the various parenting paradigms and consider them in light of the above. Previously, the "old-school" paradigm for parenting at its most extreme was that children should not be heard or seen – and that their feelings did not matter. Children were just supposed to be quiet and stay in the background and not disturb the adults. That's pretty much how it was when I grew up. And countless generations before mine have been brought up with that mindset. Today the pendulum has swung to the opposite extreme. In many families today, children are treated as if they are the center of the universe and no one else exists besides them. And they learn from an early age, that everyone else's job is to serve them and please them. Other people don't matter and no one else's feelings are important.

It's worth pointing out and meditating on the fact that both of these parenting paradigms are unhealthy and dysfunctional. Because both of these extreme parenting modes demonstrate a basic lack of respect for everyone's right to be here, exist and have their own unique feelings and experience of life. In short, in a healthy, well-functioning world with healthy, well-functioning families, both children and parents matter. Everyone matters and everyone should be treated with respect.

Good points to remember

To summarize, here are some good points to remember when it comes to being a sane, realistic parent – especially as your children grow older and become teenagers.

- Practice RESPECT. Respect for every human being's right – including your children's rights – to be who they are.
- Communicate clearly what the basic democratic principles are and what the ground rules in the home are – and explain the consequences of not behaving respectfully and/or not following the ground rules.
- Clear, respectful communications and healthy boundaries are the key to healthy interactions in every family.
- Everyone wants to be free (including your children). It's the universal urge in us all. No one fights to be a slave.

- Again, encourage every family member to respect each family member's right to be who he or she is. And this doesn't mean you can't set limits and take care of your children when they are small.
- As children grow older, let go and respect and trust in their intelligence.
- Your children didn't come into this world to make you happy (that's your job).
- It's not your job to make your children happy (that's their job).
- Children came into this world to live their own lives (that's their job).
- You came into this world to live your own life (that's your job).
- You can't know what your child's dream is. You are probably having a hard enough time figuring out what your own dream is.
- You can't know what's best for your child. Can you even know what's best for you?
- Your child has a right to be who he or she is – and experience the consequences. This does not mean that you cannot set limits in your home.
- This also does not mean you cannot explain to your children and show them through your words and actions that everything we say and do has consequences.
- You cannot prevent your children experiencing the consequences of their thoughts, words and actions. This is the setup in this Life experience and the sooner children learn this, the better.
- You cannot prevent your children from making what you may think are "mistakes". How else can they learn about life? How did you learn about life?
- Everyone is evolving and is on a learning curve, including you and your children. (See Healthy Model No. 15: *Life Is*

a Learning Curve and We Are All Evolving.)

- There is no one right answer or solution for everyone, including for your kids.
- Again practice RESPECT, RESPECT, RESPECT!

In addition, it's okay to show your kids that you're not perfect, which is the reality. And to show them that you don't know all the answers, which is also the reality. The fact that Life can sometimes be difficult for parents is something that most kids figure out even if their parents are desperately trying to hide the fact and are pretending that they have everything under control (no one does). So it's a much kinder and more relaxing way to live for everyone involved if parents allow children to see that they don't have all the answers and that life can be challenging – because this is the human condition. So an important part of being a sane, healthy parent is the ability to help children gain a more realistic view of Life and its challenges. This translates into showing children that even if Life is challenging at times, most of us are doing the best we can to figure things out – an attitude which tends to help everyone relax and take the drama and anxiety out of everyday living. (For more about this see Healthy Model No. 15: *Life Is a Learning Curve and We Are All Evolving* and Healthy Model No. 16: *Moderation*.)

When we try to follow our integrity and be as respectful and kind human beings as we can, we are automatically setting relatively sane examples for our children to learn from. Which is the best any of us can do. Moreover, this is not only a sane and realistic way to live in general, but also a sane, realistic way of interacting with the young human beings who are in our care for some years.

Happy parenting!

Healthy Model No. 15

Life Is a Learning Curve and We Are All Evolving

Every human being is evolving which means we are all on a learning curve – no matter who we are and what we do. The reality is that each one of us starts out where we start out and evolves from there. No matter who we are talking about – or where each person is on their Life journey – Life itself is all about evolution and each person is learning, growing and evolving as they go along. This is why I say, Life is a learning curve and we are all evolving.

So let's look at the mechanism. If Life is a learning curve and we are all evolving, how does it work? What is the mechanism? Well take a look around you and you will discover that no one is born with a little guidebook in their back pocket which says this is what you – John or Marie or Sandy or Michael – need to do to feel good and live a happy life. It just doesn't work that way. Each person is born into a family and that is each person's unique starting point in this particular Life adventure. Then each of us learns the belief systems and programs of our parents and then we go to school and learn more belief systems and various skills like how to read and write. But there's no one around who can teach you or me or anyone else specifically how to live a happy life. That's something each one of us has to figure out on our own. We each have to figure out what it takes for each of us to feel a little bit better and head in the direction of the happiness we each are seeking. And how do we do that? How do we find out what "feels" good to us and what doesn't? There's only one way. We can only figure out how things "feel" by trying them out. That's how we each learn what feels good to each one of us. This means that no matter who you are or where you are in your individual Life journey, the only way you can figure things out is to try things out. That's the setup here in this Life existence.

This is why it's a good idea to recognize this mechanism if you want to feel a little more comfortable about your Life experience and better understand what you and the people around you are experiencing. So our Healthy Model is as follows: Life itself is all about evolution and each person is on a learning curve. In addition, because each one of us is a separate human being with different starting points and different backgrounds, each one of us is evolving from our own unique starting point based on the conditions and circumstances of our lives and environment (both inner and outer). So regardless of who we are or where we are, we are all different and it's never over. So how does this play out in real life?

It means no matter how old we are or where we began, the nature of our Life experience continues to be evolution. And each one of us continues to learn. This means that even if you or I made what seemed like good choices for ourselves when we were 20 or 30 years old, by the time we're 40 or 50, we might be tired of those choices or have outgrown them and be ready for something new. So here's another aspect of the fact that we're all evolving – *there's no final solution!* There's no final solution for you, me or anyone – no perfect answer for any of us because things keep changing and we keep changing and evolving.

So again a better question is: how do we learn as we grow and evolve? How does it work most specifically? What is the mechanism? And as you can see from our discussion, the answer is we learn by trying things out and noticing what feels best, until that choice gets boring and then we're ready to try something new again. This is the mechanism no matter who you are or what the situation is. As a result, when it comes to choosing a career path, you do one kind of work or follow one career path until you decide to do something else. And it's the same when you buy a house or an apartment; you live there until you feel like moving somewhere else. And it's the same with our partners; people come together for a while and then they grow and change and get tired of each other and move on to new partners. That's just the way of it. It's never over. There's no final solution.

No "mistakes"!

This is where the next important bit comes in – it is impossible to make a so-called "mistake"!

Since we are all on a learning curve and all the time adjusting our behavior and choices and actions to reflect who we are and where we each are on our Life journeys, it's just not possible to make "mistakes". This is because the reality is that Life is all about learning and adjusting and all the time trying to align with what feels best for each one of us at each given moment in time. Therefore, mistakes are just not possible. But so many people are really worried about making "mistakes". I hear this all the time when coaching people. Some people are obsessed with the thought and fear that their whole life will be ruined if – God forbid – they make a so-called mistake! But now that we understand we are all evolving, we can relax a little and ask ourselves… is it really possible to make a mistake?

What do people mean by a mistake anyway? According to the dictionary a mistake is "an action or judgment that is misguided or wrong." I would suggest we even question this dictionary definition and ask for more specific information such as… what does the dictionary mean by "misguided or wrong"? And "misguided" or "wrong" according to whom? Who gets to set the standard? Who's the judge? Who gets to decide what's right and wrong for you or for me? It is important to understand that this dictionary definition is also based on the idea that there is a so-called "right" or "wrong" way to live and do things. And again – if there is – according to whom?

This is why I would suggest a healthier model for living and a more realistic approach to our Life experience is to understand that we can only learn and grow and evolve by trying things out. When something doesn't work out or isn't life-supporting or doesn't feel good to us, well then we've learned that that just is not for us... We could also say that because everything we say and do has consequences, life is a self-correcting mechanism. If it wasn't, how else could we learn?

What's for breakfast?

Here's an example of what I mean by how we learn in this life. Let's say you've just spent the night at a wonderful hotel and now it's morning and you go down to the dining room for breakfast. There is a huge breakfast buffet, a long table, which offers everything the heart could possibly desire for breakfast. There are scrambled eggs and bacon or sausages and hard-boiled eggs and soft-boiled eggs and muesli and milk and various kinds of cereal and several types of yogurt and sour cream and wonderful rolls and bread and muffins and all kind of cheeses and butter and marmalade and jams and fruit galore like grapefruit, oranges, bananas, apples, plus all sorts of other exotic fruits that you've never seen before. And then of course there is coffee and tea and orange juice and grapefruit juice and milk and... well the assortment just goes on and on. And as you stand there in line, you contemplate this abundance, and when it's your turn, you know exactly what you are going to have. You've decided on a soft-boiled egg, some muesli and fruit with milk, and a muffin with jam. Plus orange juice and coffee.

Now how did you know what to choose? How did you know what you wanted for breakfast today? You knew because, in fact, you have already tasted most of the items on the table at some time in your life, so you know that you don't like scrambled eggs and bacon or sausages and you know that you don't want cheese right now... in other words, you have tried all these things out before and you know what pleases you and what doesn't. If you hadn't tasted all these foods before, you would not be able to choose. You can't just stand there and look at the food on this breakfast table and know what you like. You have to actually try the food and taste it. Because you can't know what scrambled eggs and bacon or sausage taste like if you haven't tried them. And the same goes for whether or not you choose coffee or tea. You've tried coffee and tea so you know what they taste like and what you like or dislike. And this goes for everyone. Everyone has to taste the food to figure out whether they like a certain food or not. Just because your best friend likes coffee, it doesn't mean you like coffee. And it's pretty much the same with all of life, which is just like a huge breakfast buffet. You have to taste the different dishes in order to figure out what tastes good to you. Not what tastes good to the guy next to you in line, but to you.

And remember, when you taste something you don't like, you don't say you made a horrible "mistake", you know you've just learned that this particular dish is not for you. You know that's how it works. And then you go on to something else. And it's pretty much the same for all of Life. We have to try things out to figure out whether or not they "taste" good to us.

Everything we think, say and do has consequences

It is also true as I mentioned above that even though there are no such things as so-called "mistakes", everything we say and do has consequences. We have to keep reminding ourselves of this because this is just the setup here in this Life experience. If you go left, it has certain consequences, and if you go right, that too has certain consequences. But again, calling certain consequences a "mistake" is probably not the most constructive way to regard or define the results of any activity. It is more realistic and constructive to realize that making choices is a learning process and a learning tool for us. And that we learn by looking at and experiencing the consequences of our choices and actions. That's just how it works. That's just the setup in this life experience. And so we discover that some people, choices and activities just "feel" better than others because they are more constructive and life-giving than others. In general, we learn as we evolve that aligning with higher principles and the higher energy fields of love, compassion, respect, tolerance, and integrity just feels better. (For more about this mechanism see Healthy Model No. 7: *You Have an Inner Compass* and Healthy Model No. 12: *The Difference Between Essence and Form (Appearance)*.)

Happy learning!

Healthy Model No. 16

Moderation

As we grow and mature, we all discover that Life is never simple, it's always complicated. No matter who we are and where we find ourselves on our journey of self-development and self-realization. That's just the way it is. Life is complicated. That's "getting real" about the human condition. All human beings face challenges; all human beings face difficulties from time to time. Again, that's just the way it is. Plus, because of this, we are all evolving – that too is just the way it is.

When we begin to understand all this, we also begin to develop a little more tolerance and understanding of the human condition. This is to say, we begin to better realize what it means to be a human being. As a result, we recognize that no one is perfect and that there are no perfect solutions or final solutions that solve everything instantaneously for everyone for all times. It just doesn't work that way. It's simply not a realistic expectation when it comes to this Life experience. And if you have such unrealistic expectations to Life, sooner or later, you will be sorely disappointed. Therefore, it's a good idea to "get real" about being a human being and what the human condition involves. When we do this, we develop an excellent quality which I call "moderation". And this quality called moderation involves being a little more reasonable and realistic in terms of our expectations to ourselves and to other people, and to the human condition in general. When this happens, we are beginning to wake up to the way things actually are. We are beginning to see Life as it actually is. And as a result, we can gradually stop beating our heads against the stone wall of our own impossible and unrealistic expectations to Life, to other people and to ourselves. This doesn't mean we can't have goals and want to improve ourselves and our lives. No, that's not what this is about. What it does mean is that we are just more realistic about what Life is and what this means for us and for everyone else. Moreover, we have a better understanding of what we can actually do something about (not much) and what we can't do anything about (most things and especially most other people).

What does moderation actually look like?

So how does this moderation play out in our daily lives? What does it actually look like? To begin with, when we begin to have a more moderate view and a better understanding of this thing called Life, we are no longer such perfectionists. Perfectionism is a form of illness actually – a form of mental delusion – because it has nothing to do with reality. "Perfect" doesn't exist – and if it did – who would get to define what "perfect" is? This is why perfectionism drives people crazy. Because perfectionism means that people are all the time resisting the way things are and trying to achieve the impossible. This is a highly stressful way to live. Both for oneself and for the people around one.

Moral scrupulosity is pretty much the same. Moral scrupulosity is another example of what happens when we have standards of behavior that are extremely unrealistic in terms of being a human being. It is when we expect ourselves and others to always live up to some arbitrary standards of right and wrong that do not tolerate or factor in what being a human being is all about. And again, this is a very stressful way to live and has nothing to do with being tolerant, wise, kind and able to embrace oneself and all of our fellow human beings. Moral scrupulosity is quite the opposite and does not factor in the reality which is that we are all learning and evolving – each and every one of us. This also means that we all think, say and do things which are not always the best or wisest course of action in relation to the given situation. But then again, who gets to judge – and who can see the end of all things? No one – right?!

Another characteristic of moderation is that we no longer think so much in terms of either/or. In other words, our thinking is not so black and white anymore. It's not, either I'm perfect or I'm a fiasco. It's not either I know all the answers or I'm a total idiot. Again, we begin to take a more moderate view of things and we realize that Life itself is more nuanced. We begin to see that reality is usually somewhere in the middle, which translates into, "Well, I might not be perfect, but neither is anyone else. And like everyone else, I also have my strengths and weaknesses." So moderation can sound like "– Yes it's true, I don't have all the answers, but I'm reasonably intelligent and can probably figure this out if I just relax a bit and give myself a chance."

So again, moderation is a more relaxed, easygoing attitude to life. When you are more moderate, you don't freak out so much about things, people or situations. You're not such a drama queen anymore. Moreover, you are much more able to take one day at a time and assess the various situations that arise a little more realistically.

And guess what? Being more moderate about Life just feels a whole lot better. This is just a much nicer and more enjoyable way to live. So moderation actually shows itself to us by the fact that we usually feel "moderately happy" or "moderately comfortable" in our daily lives, which again is a lovely and enjoyable way to live.

Good questions to ask yourself

In terms of moderation, here are some questions you might want to ask yourself to check how you are doing in terms of having a little more nuanced view of life. And also to help you identify what areas you might need to work on and be a little more aware of:

- Do you understand that life is complicated and can be challenging for everyone?
- How realistic is your assessment of the human condition?
- Do you understand that no one (including yourself) is perfect?
- What is your relationship to making so-called "mistakes"? Do you understand that thinking, saying and doing things that might not be so wise or appropriate in a given situation are part of the human condition and are, in fact, the way we learn?
- Are you a drama queen? Or are you beginning to understand that things aren't so black and white?
- And what about generalizations? Can you see that reality is usually more nuanced? It's almost never "always" or "never", but rather "sometimes".
- Do you feel that your life situation is highly stressful or do you have a more easygoing attitude to Life and the challenges we all face?
- Are you generally moderately happy or moderately comfortable in your life, or are you angry, irritated, and sad a lot of the time?
- Do you have unrealistic expectations to yourself and to other people, or have you learned to moderate your expectations to be a little more in alignment with reality?
- Can you see that it's your thinking that determines your experience?
- And if so, can you investigate your own beliefs in terms of the areas in your life where you feel unhappy or stressed? (For more about how to identify and question your beliefs, see Healing Process No. 6 about how to explore *The Difference Between Reality and Your Expectations*.)
- Can you take the so-called "bumps on the road" in your stride?
- Can you say to yourself, "Okay this might be unpleasant

or challenging, but it's not dangerous and I'll probably figure it out"?

- In other words, are you less extreme – less catastrophic – in your assessment of situations?
- Are you less judgmental when it comes to other people because you now realize that you can't possibly know what's going on inside of another person?
- Can you also see that you can't possibly know what's best for someone else? It's hard enough to figure out what's best for yourself.

When you consider the concept of moderation, if you discover that you still have unrealistic expectations to yourself and Life and to other people – what can you do about it? To begin with, read and study the Basic Observations in the next section of this book. And then read them again until you have started to integrate this understanding and these observations into your daily way of viewing and approaching Life. Once you really have understood and digested the basic mechanisms about the way Life actually operates, you will find that you automatically begin to adjust your behavior and that you can navigate a little more easily and wisely through Life. Mainly because you discover that you gradually stop trying to do or control things that are beyond your control. In other words, you are becoming more realistic and moderate in your expectations. And this is what moderation is all about – getting real about what you can actually do something about.

It's also good to remember that moderation, like everything else, is something we develop gradually. So keep reminding yourself of the truths about the way Life is, and enjoy the fact that each day you are slowly but surely becoming a little more moderate in your assessment of Life and of being a human being.

Functional	Dysfunctional
Based on reality	Based on flawed premises
Life supporting	Not life supporting
Body goes strong	Body goes weak
Comfort	Discomfort
Energy system balanced	Energy system out of balance
Flow	Blockage or resistance
Ease	Dis-ease
Clarity	Confusion
Respect	Lack of respect
Inherent worth	Performance-based worth
Inner Compass	Looking to others for guidance
Healthy boundaries	Boundary violating
Responsible for oneself	Blaming others
Assertive	Passive or aggressive
Learning curve	Perfectionism
Realistic	Unrealistic expectations
Democracy	Tyranny / inequality
Allows and accepts diversity	Intolerance / conformity
Accepts life	Resists life
Truth	Falsehood
Healthy models	Unhealthy behavior
Constructive	Destructive
Moderation	Black and white thinking
Based on principle	Based on content, opinions
True Power (inner condition)	Force (trying to manipulate outer conditions)

Part 2

Some Basic Observations About This Thing Called Life

Introduction

Some Basic Observations About the Nature of Life

If you want to live a happy life, it is vitally important that you have a relatively realistic assessment of this thing called Life because then you can be more realistic about the things in your life which you actually can do something about – as well as about the things in your life which are beyond your control. This is why understanding some of the basic principles or characteristics of Life, i.e. the Nature of Reality, is so vitally important. And that is what this section of this book is about and why I call this information – Some Basic Observations about Life. These Basic Observations describe the setup here, the way Life is, and the impersonal mechanisms or principles behind the way things are.

When you understand these observations and have confirmed them for yourself – through your own observation – then you will be able to use this information to live more wisely and happily.

In brief there are three main reasons why these Basic Observations are so important.

- We cannot change the way things are – we cannot change the setup here in this world – here in Life. It is what it is. Life is what it is.
- We can navigate more wisely through Life when we understand the setup and the way things are. In other words, when we understand some of the basic, impersonal mechanisms or Laws of the Universe.
- And finally: We will have a more realistic idea of what we can do something about and, as a result, what is not in our power to change.

The way things are

Let's start by looking at some of the things that everyone (you and I and everyone else) can observe and confirm for ourselves. Let's look carefully at this thing called "Life" and see what we can identify as qualities or characteristics, which are universal, impersonal and which apply to everyone. Qualities or characteristics that everyone can confirm for themselves.

I would ask you to really think about this and observe the things I am going to point out until you can confirm these Basic Observations for yourself and are absolutely satisfied that this is the way things are. Once you have understood these Basic Observations, this understanding will automatically begin to change the way you think, act and react in the world as you move about in your daily life. And as a result, you will experience more ease and flow in your daily Life experiences, and you will be able to live a little bit more sanely and happily.

You will also discover that our Basic Democratic Rights and Principles and the Healthy Models in Part 1 of this book are all based on a deep understanding of these Basic Observations.

So here comes a quick rundown of some Basic Observations about the way things are – about the setup in this Life experience.

Observation 1

There Is "Reality" and Then There Is Your Thinking about Reality

This is one of the most important Basic Observations. A fundamental observation that can and will transform the way you look at the world and the way you experience everything. And the observation is: There is this thing called "Life", which I call "reality", and then there is your thinking. And they are not the same. They are two different things.

So let's slow it all down and look a little more carefully at this statement.

What do I mean by "reality"? By reality, I mean the things that happen in your life – the situations, people, circumstances and events that manifest or arise in your life. This is what I mean by reality. So that is one thing. The things that happen – that's reality.

And then there is your thinking about the things that happen. And that's another thing. So again, slowly... things happen. In other words, people come and go, situations arise and disappear, and then there is the way you think about or regard the things that happen in your life. In other words, there is the way you relate to, interpret or think about what is going on. There is the way you think about the people, events and circumstances that are arising in your life.

These are two different things. There's what happens and then there is what you think about the things that are happening and how you relate to or interpret what is happening. This is a crucial observation. And vitally important to notice and understand if you want to achieve any degree of self-determination, control and happiness in your life. Therefore, I would ask you kindly to take the time to observe this and confirm for yourself that this is true.

Confirm for yourself that "reality" or the events and situations in your life are one thing – these events, situations and people come and go. And the way you interpret these events, situations and people is another thing.

It's also important to notice here that because reality and our thinking about reality are two different things, if there is one situation or event and 10 different people present at the same event or situation, you can have 10 different interpretations of the exact same event.

Now why is this important to notice?

Because it is our thinking – our interpretation – of events and people that determines our experience of life.

Your Thinking Determines Your Experience of What Is Going On – Not What Is Going On

Yes, this is the next crucial observation – that it is our thinking – in other words, our interpretation of events and people that determines our experience of life.

This is so important to notice and understand because at present, most people on the planet believe that something happens out there (in other words, an event or situation arises or a person appears), and that this phenomenon is the cause of their experience. They believe that because "this" or "that" happened, this or that is the reason why they are sad or happy – or depressed or overjoyed. Or they believe that "this" happened and that's why they are so stressed or frustrated or disappointed. They have not yet understood that there is a difference between what is actually happening and how they think about or relate to what is happening.

But here's what's really going on: Things happen and then you interpret what this event or circumstance means for you. The short version is: Something happens and you think it's good – then you're pretty happy. Or something happens and you think it's less good – then you are less happy. Again, we have to slow things down so we can see this chain of events. Until we can observe for ourselves the mechanism:

A situation, event or person --> your thinking about this situation, event or person --> your reaction or how you experience this situation --> how you feel

Unfortunately, most people today are unconscious of this

mechanism so they believe that something happens in their life – "something out there" – and that this "something out there" is the cause of their experience. They have not yet understood that there is something going on between the event and how we feel – and that middle step is our thinking and our interpretation of what the event means for us.

You can test this observation for yourself by noticing that if 10 people are present at the same event or are in the same exact situation and something happens – in all probability you will have 10 different reactions and experiences. In other words, 10 different reactions or experiences of the exact same situation or event. So please watch closely and notice how differently people react to the exact same event, situation or person.

Let's take a simple example. You go to a party. There are 50 people at the party. It's the same situation, the same party for everyone. The same people are there, the same music, the same food, the same surroundings. But if you look closely, you will see that not everyone experiences the party in the same way. One person thinks it's the best party they've ever been to, another finds it boring or mediocre, another feels lonely because he/she is missing their partner, another feels shy and stands in a corner or has an anxiety attack. Hence, in principle, there are 50 possible different experiences of the exact same party…

The same goes for the various challenges we meet in life. Take for example a work situation. Let's say your boss asks you to be in charge of an important project. Now what does this mean? The reality is that this is a work assignment. It's a project. But people can, and most probably will, react very differently to getting an assignment like this. Why? Because getting an assignment like this can, and does, mean different things to different people. For one person, heading the project will seem overwhelming and the person will almost immediately experience a lot of stress. Because that's how they interpret the situation. They think it's "important" and they might feel anxious about their skills or ability to perform as expected. For another person, heading the project may feel entirely different. Perhaps he or she might feel like it's going to be great fun and this person likes the idea of being challenged and trusted with the task. So in this case, the person will then experience renewed energy and joy at work. In both cases, the event was the same – a work assignment to head a project. But because different people have very different interpretations of their abilities, skills and what the situation requires of them, they will also have very different experiences of what getting this assignment means and thus they will react differently.

Observation 3

Your Thinking and Belief Systems Are Formed By Your Background

Now we might ask – if it's true that our thinking determines our experience – then what determines our thinking? Again, we have to slow things down and look carefully at reality. When we do, we discover there are a million different factors and influences that have made you, me, and everyone else think and feel the way we do. There are a million different factors and influences that make you interpret events and situations and circumstances in just the way you do.

Here are some of them.

Your thinking or belief systems are formed by a multitude of factors such as your background and level of consciousness at birth, the family you grew up in, your parents and their belief systems, the country you live in, the religion you have, your gender (or rather gender-specific programming), the education you have, your friends, the neighborhood you grew up in, the neighborhood you live in now, the social media contacts you have and have had, the television programs you have watched and are watching, the movies you have seen, the books you have read, and all the other millions of influences you have experienced along your pathway in life so far. Again, each one of us is unique in this way. No two people are exactly the same, because no two people have exactly the same combination of influences or background – even people who grew up in the same family. Each one of us is completely unique and the singular result of a myriad of varying influences that shaped our thinking and our belief systems, starting from a very early age – from the moment we were born actually.

Again it is important to slow down and actually observe how

this happens. It's easy for most of us to see this if we consider how babies are. Babies are born into this world without the programs or belief systems that each individual person slowly learns in their childhood. In other words, babies are innocent as far as their consciousness is concerned. They don't yet believe all the thousand and one things we each get programmed to believe even though each child has the level of consciousness he or she was born with. But once a child is born, it gets programmed with the thousand and one ideas or arbitrary rules about good and bad behavior and what's right and wrong that most people are unconsciously trained or conditioned to believe.

Just think, for example, about your parents. What were their belief systems and how did these people and their belief systems form and influence the thinking and belief systems you have today? Can you identify some of your parents' basic beliefs? Did they believe Life is hard, a struggle, and that money doesn't grow on trees? Did they believe you were lucky if you got a break? Or were they optimistic and positive people? Did they believe in you and your ability to succeed in Life? Did they try to instill a sense of self-confidence and hopefulness in you? Did they tell you that they trusted in your intelligence and talents? Did they say they were confident that you would find your way in life and have a happy, healthy life experience? Or were they more pessimistic about you and Life in general and of your chances of living a good life? Did they see difficulties everywhere they turned? Did they complain and worry a lot? And how did all of this influence you? Did you ever think about this? Did you ever really contemplate how you were programmed in your childhood – probably without your ever noticing it? It's a really good idea to slow things down and ask yourself questions like these because then you will be able to see more clearly why you think and react the way you do today. Plus you will be able to see more clearly that this is true for everyone else too. Everyone you meet along your pathway is also thinking and reacting based on their background and belief systems – in short, based on the way they were programmed.

Unfortunately, most people on the planet today are unconscious of this mechanism. They think what they believe is "right" is right! They think what they learned in school is correct. They think that this is just the way things are. They are not yet conscious of the fact that they have been programmed from an early age to believe certain ideas – and to discard or reject other ideas. And because they have not yet learned about these basic mechanisms of mind, they have not yet discovered that they can also question the validity of these beliefs and what they are thinking and believing. Unfortunately, most people can't yet see whether or not their beliefs have anything to do with reality.

But when we begin to observe this and can start to see the mechanism of how everyone gets programmed, then we can also begin to identify our belief systems and how we got them. And this is the key to change. Because when we can see what's going on, we can also begin to ask ourselves if the belief systems we have been programmed with have anything to do with reality. In addition, we can ask ourselves if these beliefs are now serving us well in our adult lives. In other words, are these beliefs realistic? Are they healthy and sane? And do they contribute to our happiness and well-being in this Life experience?

Observation 4

The Only Meaning Anything Has, Is the Meaning You Give It

So now we're starting to get it – we are starting to understand that Life is a purely subjective experience. Each one of us is living in our own mental universe. Things happen, and the only meaning anything has for you or for me or for anyone else, is the meaning we give it. Radical and revolutionary as this may seem, it is true nevertheless. So please meditate on this observation – over and over again. Please contemplate this radical truth. If you want to be free, if you want to liberate yourself and live the happy, satisfying life you dream of living, please think about this and constantly remind yourself of this radical truth and all the implications it has – *the only meaning anything has, is the meaning you give it!*

Wow! Can you get a sense, a small sense, of what this actually means for you? Talk about self-empowerment!

Can you see that this is the key to freedom! Can you see that this is the key to living a happy life? This is the key to setting yourself free from being dependent on other people or outside events or on specific circumstances in order to be happy. This is the key, the understanding, that not only sets you free, but also allows you to take your personal power back.

So please think about this, please contemplate this and dwell on this every day. And watch how your experience of life changes in every now moment.

This is not to say there are no collective belief systems or collective experiences, because there are. In fact, because the nature of consciousness is innocent and every child is born innocent, with a consciousness that accepts whatever it is presented with, this also means that everyone is innocently programmed. Everyone is innocently indoctrinated from birth, everyone automatically learns the belief systems of their parents, family, friends, and their environment. But because most people are unconscious of this mechanism, they are unaware of this. And so they are unable to identify and question the belief systems they learned as children – belief systems which will continue to run and operate in their adult lives. And many of these beliefs are what we call the collective belief systems. They are the unquestioned beliefs that almost everyone innocently adopts. So yes, there are collective – or commonly held – belief systems, which most individuals believe. And it is these so-called collective belief systems which are the cause of the so-called collective experience, which involves most people.

What specifically do I mean by collective belief systems? I mean the concrete and specific things most people are automatically thinking and saying all day long. All you have to do is listen to the conversation of almost anyone you meet and you will hear phrase after phrase of unquestioned beliefs such as:

- That's just what happens when you get older.
- Family is important.
- You need a partner to be happy.
- Children should love their parents.
- Parents should love their children.
- Money doesn't grow on trees.
- Life is a struggle.
- No gain without pain.
- The body just falls apart when we get older.
- Allergies run in families.
- It's hereditary.
- It's all about genes. (It's genetic so there's nothing we can do about it.)
- We need to save the world.

- The world needs saving.
- You can't trust anyone.
- One in five people get it, so there's a good chance I will get it too.
- It's the flu season.
- It's his fault. It's her fault. It's their fault. It's someone's fault.
- You can always count on your family.
- Kids are like that.
- Mothers should understand their children.
- You should respect your elders.
- After 40 it's all downhill.
- After 50 it's all downhill.
- After 60 it's all downhill.
- Life is dangerous.
- Death is dangerous.
- It's dangerous to make a mistake.
- Money and success are a sign of intelligence.
- Everyone needs a partner to be happy.
- It's incurable. There's nothing you can do about it.
- Decline just happens naturally.
- Teenagers are like that.
- Boys are like that.
- Girls are like that.
- Children can't be friends with their parents.
- It runs in the family.
- There's a right way and a wrong way to do things.
- Divorce is terrible for the children.
- Middle age is like that.
- It's a midlife crisis.
- It's the government's fault.
- The weather is to blame.
- The flu season always comes when the weather turns cold.

- It's because you're 20 or 30 or 40 or 50 or 60 or 70…
- You can't just do what you want.
- Men shouldn't be so emotional.
- Women are so emotional.
- Everyone needs to go on holiday.
- It's not good to work on weekends.
- It's important to spend time with the family.

These are just some examples of the common beliefs of most people. And by this I mean beliefs that most people just accept as being true without questioning whether or not they have anything to do with reality. Without questioning whether or not such beliefs are inherent characteristics of the nature of Life itself.

This is also why, when we stop and look at the above thoughts and beliefs, we discover that so many of them are actually quite painful because they do not reflect, and are not in alignment with, the Nature of Reality. In other words, they do not reflect the setup of this thing called Life, so when we believe them we feel discomfort. Because our Inner Compass is letting us know that these beliefs are, in fact, not in harmony with the way things are.

It is also interesting to note in this connection that statistics are really just a description – or you could say the out-picturing – of the collective belief systems of humanity. Because thanks to the power of the mind, we get what we believe we're going to get. (See Healing Process No. 7 on *Using the Power of Mind Wisely for Healing and Recovery*.) Therefore because of this mechanism – that we get what we believe we are going to get – most people believe the manifestation is the "proof" of the truth of the statistics. But this is not what is really going on. Statistics are actually just the manifestation of what so many people are holding in mind. Statistics are actually a clear demonstration of the power of our minds. But unfortunately, as I said in the beginning of this section, most people are still unaware of how the power of the mind determines our experience.

But now you are waking up to this mechanism. And this means that just because most people still unconsciously buy into the collective belief systems of their families, religion, group, country – it doesn't mean you have to. When you are able to identify and understand the mechanism and question these beliefs and belief systems for yourself, you will discover that you don't have to believe what everyone else believes. You don't have to buy into the collective belief systems, which means you can have a completely different experience than everyone else. So regardless of what everyone else is thinking, believing and experiencing, you can take control of your own thinking and learn more and more how to determine what you experience on a daily basis. Pretty neat, isn't it...

Observation 5

"We" Are Separate Individuals

Here is another vital Basic Observation. "We" human beings are separate; "we" are separate individuals. Have you noticed? We're not joined together with anyone else at the hip. You are you and I am me and this goes for everyone. In addition, each one of us is inside of ourselves, experiencing the world from the inside out. In other words, you're in you. You're inside you and you have your own thoughts and feelings and your own experience of this thing called Life. And I'm me and I'm inside me and I have my own thoughts and feelings and my own experience of this thing called Life. And there's no immediate connection between what I'm experiencing and what you're experiencing, even if we are lying in bed together entwined. You're still experiencing Life from inside you and I'm still experiencing Life from inside me. Thus we see that each one of us is a unique focal point in the Infinite field of consciousness. This is really important to notice and understand. (For an in-depth look at the nature of consciousness, see my books *The Awakening Human Being – A Guide to the Power of Mind* and *The Mental Laws – Understanding the Way the Mind Works*.)

Observation 6

Each Person Is Completely Unique

When we understand that we are separate individuals and that each individual's thoughts and belief systems are formed and determined by their individual background (family, culture, country, religion, gender, etc.), as well as each person's level of consciousness at birth, we can also see that each individual is unique. No two people are alike. Everyone has his or her own unique spin on life. Everyone. And everyone is having their own unique subjective experience of this thing called Life. Why? Again because each person has his or her own unique belief system and thinking patterns, which determine each person's experience.

Just think about this and notice and you will discover that this is true even of people in the same family. Brothers and sisters, for example. Kids in the same family – with the same mother and father – living under the same roof, eating the same food, going to the same school – each one of them is also having very different life experiences. They can even have very different ideas about what they want, like, feel, no matter how similar their surroundings might seem to be. So take the time to notice and understand this until you can confirm for yourself that this is the Nature of Reality, that this is the setup here in this Life. It has nothing to do with you; it's just the way things are.

So just look around.

Then notice that this is even true of people who are partners and who live together and love each other very much. Even if they share the same bed and are physically intimate, they still have different ideas, different thoughts, different feelings – and different experiences. And even very often *very* different experiences – as anyone in a couple relationship knows!

This is so important to keep in mind when dealing with other people and as we navigate through Life. Each one of us is a unique creation of Life itself, which is also why no two people have the same fingerprints. This is also why no one size fits all. Which means there is no universal answer or universal solution that works equally well for everyone. Because each person is where he or she is and is living life from his or her own unique vantage point.

Understanding that this is reality, is also the basis of our democratic societies – that each person has the right to be who he or she is and where he or she is in their path of evolution through Life, because that's the way things are. That's the setup – each person is who they are and is where they are. Each person is unique and experiencing Life from his or her own unique vantage perspective. (See Healthy Model No. 1 about democracy for more.)

Which leads us to our next Basic Observation.

Observation 7

You Can't Get Inside Another Person and Think or Feel for That Person

Here's another really important Basic Observation. You can't get inside another person and think or feel for that person. It is obvious now that you know the setup. But I am sure you have tried – because we all have. We have all tried, at some point in time in our Life journey, to control the thinking of another person, be it a parent or partner or child. And we've failed completely. Have you noticed? And if not, please do. Just notice that you can't get inside another person's head. It's just not possible. Which means you can't get inside another person's head and think and feel for that person, no matter how hard you try. And the reverse is true too. No one else can get inside your head and think and feel for you, no matter how hard they try.

So this is another very important Basic Observation. A Basic Observation which is very important to notice and to remember. Why? Because this leads us to our next Basic Observation.

Observation 8

You Can't "Fix" or Control or Change Another Person

When you understand that everyone is unique and that you can't get inside another person and think or feel for that person, you can then also understand that you can't "fix" or control or change another person. Period. No matter how well-meaning your intentions may be. No matter how much you love the person, no matter how much you want to protect the other person from discomfort or difficulties, we simply can't fix, control or change other people. It's just not possible. That's the deal. That's the setup here. It's not up to you. It's not your job. Which is a very important thing for most of us to "get real" about. Why? Because so many people spend so much time and energy trying to "fix" or "change" or "convince" or "manipulate" other people into doing what they believe is best or the right thing to do. And it's always a hopeless project. Hopeless!

I hear about this all the time in my private sessions with people. How people honestly believe that someone (parent, child, mate) would be so much better off if they would just get with the program (which is their program). Then the other person would be happy and everything would be hunky-dory. But when you know the laws of the Universe and understand the setup here, you realize that it's never, ever going to happen. So if you want to live a little bit more sanely and happily, it's a good idea to meditate on these Basic Observations. Because when you meditate on these Observations, you can begin to understand what you can change and what you can't.

This doesn't mean we can't ask for what we want. Nor does it mean we can't attempt to influence other people through our words and actions – yes, of course we can. But in the final analysis, when you have made your suggestions or asked politely for what you believe is best, you can't do more than that. And that's because you cannot get into someone else's head and control their thinking, feeling or actions.

Changing is difficult

There is also another important piece of the puzzle to keep in mind here too. When you think about asking someone else to change (to make you feel better), just consider this. Just think about how hard it is for you to change – how difficult it is for you to change yourself. Just think about the fact that even if you have decided to make a change in your thinking or behavior or your life – how difficult it is to actually do. In fact, it's almost impossible for most of us to initiate change from within (like watching and being mindful of our thinking or holding our tongue or stopping smoking or whatever it is) – so to expect that someone else will easily change because we think they "should"… well that's quite a stretch. Obviously, that's not very realistic. So if you want to navigate a little more sanely in your life, I suggest "getting real" about changing other people.

This is why I always suggest in private sessions that people take note of what other people actually say and do, and then decide how they are going to relate to that. Because this is the reality of who and what this person is all about right now. Don't waste your precious life energy assuming you know what another person is really thinking or feeling or that the person is going to change at some magical moment in the future. Forget all that dream stuff and look at what's going on right in front of you. And relate to that. In other words, listen to what he or she is saying and watch what he or she is doing – and then make your decisions based on the reality of the other person's words and actions. (For more about "getting real" about other people see Healing Process No. 6 about *The Difference Between Reality and Your Expectations*.)

Seeking love and approval

Another important aspect of understanding that we can't get inside other people and think and feel for them is the realization that this means we can't make someone like us or dislike us. Whether a person likes you or dislikes you is always based on that person's thoughts, belief systems and level of consciousness. It's their deal. It really has nothing to do with you because it's their judgment, their interpretation of you which determines whether they approve of you or not. Which is why trying to please people and seeking other people's love and approval can be so painful. Because we simply can't get inside other people's heads and control what they think or feel. It's just not possible. People's reactions to you and to me and to everything else is just telling us about them and their beliefs. It's not about you or me. Mind-boggling to realize this...

Observation 9

You Cannot Make Another Person Happy – or Unhappy

When we understand these Basic Observations and especially Basic Observation 2 that – *our thinking determines our experience, not outer circumstances or events* – we can also understand that another person's happiness or unhappiness is not the result of what we say or do. Regardless of what they tell us. Rather, we understand that each person's happiness or unhappiness is the result of that person's interpretation of what is going on in his or her life. Accordingly, we can see that happiness or unhappiness is a purely subjective experience. It's an "inside job" as I always say. Because happiness or unhappiness is based on only one thing and one thing alone – how each person views and interprets the situations and circumstances he or she is living with and in.

This is the mechanism of mind: *Our thinking determines our experience.*

This is what determines every person's experiences including yours and mine.

Things happen and then we each react according to our belief systems.

Things happen and we each react based on our background, level of consciousness, upbringing, beliefs, and practiced ways of thinking and reacting.

So each person's happiness depends on their thinking. Whether it's your partner, your child, your parents, or your friends. Their thinking determines their experience. This is the setup here – for everyone. There are no exceptions to this rule.

When we see this and understand this, we also understand that we cannot make another person happy or unhappy. Again, regardless of what they tell us. Their experience of your choices and actions is based on their belief systems and upbringing and views on life. Which doesn't mean you shouldn't be polite and treat other people with respect – of course you should, so we're not talking about that. But we are talking about you or I not being responsible for another person's happiness or unhappiness.

The opposite is also true – other people cannot be responsible for your happiness or mine. It just doesn't work that way. That's not how the Universe is set up. That's not the mechanism. Just take a look around and you will see that different people react differently to the exact same situation or circumstances. It all depends on how they interpret what's going on, and that's always a relative judgment depending on who the person is, what their beliefs are, and where they are in their lives and development.

Examples of this mechanism

Let's look at some examples of what I mean here:

Situation one: You want to go away for the weekend with your girlfriends – or you want to go away for a silent meditation retreat for the next 10 days. But your husband gets upset when you tell him. He happens to be the kind of man who expects you to be around when he needs you and do all the things he wants you to do with him. But what does that have to do with you? All this tells us is what kind of a man he is. It tells us what his belief systems are. It really has nothing to do with you. Because just think about it. In principle, he could respond quite differently and say, "How wonderful, sweetheart, I hope you have a great time." Or he could say, "That's great, I really need some time alone, too, so I'm happy you're going away." Or he could say, "Good for you, I was planning on going fishing with my buddies anyway…" Or he could say, "Do what you like!" There's just no end to how people can react to whatever you say or do. It all depends on their thoughts and beliefs – not on you.

Situation two: You ask your partner for a divorce. How does he or she react? Well again, it depends on how your partner interprets this event and what he or she thinks it's going to mean for them. Your partner could, for example, be overjoyed, because basically he/she is sick and tired of you anyway and was longing for his/her freedom. Your partner just didn't have the guts to bring up the subject! In a case like this, your request will probably be met with a hallelujah (even if it is a silent one), and without you knowing it, your partner could well be jumping up and down for joy inside, thinking it's finally over and I'm going to be free. Or your partner could be indifferent. Or blasé. Or your partner could be devastated, especially if he/she believes you are the love of his or her life and that he/she will never find another love. Or your partner could be confused, or jealous, or sad, or curious... the number of ways he or she could react to a situation like this is almost limitless.

Situation three: Your partner's family has invited you and your partner and children to their summerhouse for a week. You tell your partner you don't want to go for a week. You are willing to visit them for an afternoon, but you are not interested in staying there for a whole week. Your partner cries in dismay, "But my mother will be devastated; she's expecting us to come." What does your partner's mother have to do with you? Just because your partner's mother has certain ideas and expectations as to how families should be together, it's not up to you to fulfill her expectations. If she's disappointed, it's because of her beliefs. So it is her problem, her reaction, and basically her creation. She could just as well react with understanding – and so could your partner. Your partner could also say, "You know, darling, I actually feel the same. I guess I'll just have to pull myself together and tell my mother we're not coming. It will be such a relief to get it over with."

These are just three examples of situations where a person could feel happy or unhappy, depending on how that person interprets the situation. But when we look closely, we discover that it's actually not the situation itself which determines how the person feels about the situation. Rather, the determining factor is the way in which the person interprets the situation. In other words, the person's thinking as to what this situation means for him or her. Situations in and of themselves have no meaning, but we give them meaning by the way we regard them. The truth is – our reaction to external events is always an internal event. When we understand this, we can also see that the only one who can make anyone happy or unhappy is the person him- or herself.

Observation 10

You Are Not Responsible for Another Person's Experience

The previous Basic Observation leads us to our next Observation – that you cannot possibly be responsible for another person's experience. Obviously! When we understand the Basic Observations described in this book and begin to comprehend the mechanisms of this Life experience, it becomes so abundantly clear what's going on. We're all – each and every one of us – lost in our own dream. Each person is lost in their own very private and very personal experience of life. Each person is almost always totally identified with the Life experience he or she believes they are experiencing because of their level of consciousness and belief systems. But some of us are waking up – like you! And this is the good news.

So set yourself free – and set everyone else free!

Have confidence in other people's intelligence

In terms of who's responsible for another person's experience, it's also important to have confidence in other people's intelligence and their ability to learn, grow and change. And to recognize that it's part of each person's journey through Life to meet challenges and disappointments. The paradox is that it is often precisely these Life challenges and problems that stimulate a person to think and ask questions – and to grow and change. So when we look at challenges in this light, we can see they are almost always a good thing. Therefore, it is good to keep in mind that even if, for example, a person is sorely disappointed because of your decisions or choices, then hopefully their internal experience will stimulate them to look within at their own beliefs and patterns of thinking instead of just blaming you for their disappointment. When a person begins to look within for the cause of their own dissatisfaction or suffering, it is an important step forward in their journey of personal development. Because when this happens, it means the person, hopefully, is beginning to own their own personal power, which also involves owning their own part in any situation (whatever the situation is). For more about this significant step in a person's evolution of consciousness, see the Pyramid of Evolution in Healthy Model No. 13.

Taking responsibility is always a great step forward in any situation – and for everyone involved. Thus, we see that disappointment is often the impetus for real growth and personal development. So remember, you cannot see the end of all things (for more about this see Healthy Model No. 15: *Life Is a Learning Curve and We Are All Evolving*).

Observation 11

Other People Are Not Responsible for Your Experience

It works the other way around too. If you are not responsible for the experiences of other people, other people cannot possibly be responsible for your experiences either. Because as we are discovering, Life is a purely subjective experience for each one of us. Determined solely by our thinking and our belief systems – and our level of consciousness. Which means your experience is always the direct result of your thinking and beliefs and the way in which you relate to whatever is happening to you. This means another person cannot possibly make you happy or unhappy. But don't get me wrong; this is not to say that other people should not treat you with respect. Nor does this mean you should not have healthy boundaries or be assertive. I am not talking about that. Of course other people should treat you with respect. So we are not talking about respect here, because respect is the basis of all good human relations as we have seen in the various Healthy Models for Relationships in Part 1 of this book. Without basic respect there is no reason to be in a relationship with anyone, regardless of whether or not they are family, friends or colleagues.

What we are talking about here is that it's important to understand that blaming other people for your experience is giving your power away. When you believe that the way you feel is someone else's fault, you are basically saying that your happiness is dependent on what someone else thinks or says or does – and this is what is called the "victim" mentality. And a victim mentality makes you powerless and makes other people responsible for your happiness and life experience. Which is, obviously, the exact opposite of self-empowerment. But fortunately for us all, reality is different. Reality says it's up to you! Reality says it's all about you! So take your power back and realize that you, and you alone, are responsible for your experience of life.

For more about how you can take control of your thinking, and thus change your experience of Life (without being dependent on what other people are thinking, saying, or doing), see Healing Process No. 7: *Using the Power of Mind Wisely* as well as my books *The Road to Power – Fast Food for the Soul* and *The Awakening Human Being – A Guide to the Power of Mind*.

Observation 12

It's Not Personal!

When we "get" all this, when we understand the Basic Observations about the Nature of Life and the setup here, it's such a relief. Because then we also understand that it's not personal. Nothing is! We've been brought up to believe that if somebody says or does something when we're around, it has something to do with us. But when we understand that everyone is living in their own mental universe, thinking and reacting and experiencing because of their own level of consciousness, belief systems and thinking, then we can see, it's never about us! It's always about them. This means when someone is happy, then you know that things are harmonizing with their belief systems and worldview, and when they're unhappy or grumpy and irritated, then you know that things are not living up to their expectations about the way they think things "should" be for them to be happy. Whatever a person's reactions are, it is only showing his or her beliefs, level of consciousness, and what's going on inside them. And that's about it. It's all about them. That's all that's ever going on. What a relief to find this out. It sets you free because it means you are not responsible for how other people think or feel. What's going on with them is all about them. *It's not your fault!*

But as I keep repeating over and over in this book, this does not mean we cannot and should not treat other people with respect. Of course we can and should, quite simply, because respect is the basis of all good human relationships. Respect is the most fundamental quality of all satisfying relationships because respect is what feels best – to us and to everyone else. This is what being an integrous human being is all about. Kindness and respect. It simply feels better to be kind and respectful. It simply feels better to try to be respectful in every situation and with every person. And since feeling good is what we all want, it makes sense to treat our fellow human beings with respect. But don't get carried away and forget that self-love comes first. Loving self is the basis of all healthy behavior and all healthy relationships. And in practice, this self-love and self-respect express themselves as assertiveness, healthy boundaries and constructive communications. Trying to fix other people, however, or taking responsibility for the way other people feel or their experiences, that is not our job, it's not something we can do. That's not the setup in this Life experience. Each one of us is on our own journey of evolution and growth.

In Conclusion

So now that we know it's not personal and we can't fix other people or take responsibility for their experience of Life, what can we do something about?

We can do something about us.

We can do something about how we think, act and treat ourselves and our fellow human beings. That's what we can become more and more aware of and do something about.

In order to check our development, it is a good idea to ask ourselves the following questions on a regular basis...

- Am I following my integrity (my Inner Compass)?
- Am I doing the Highest and Best I can envision in every situation?
- Am I treating my fellow human beings with respect?
- Do I have healthy boundaries?
- Do I respect everyone's right to their feelings and opinions?
- Do I respect my own right to have all my feelings and opinions?
- Do I respect everyone's right to live their lives as they deem best?
- Am I always striving to communicate respectively and constructively with everyone I meet?
- When there is disagreement, do I make every effort to find workable compromises that the involved parties can agree to?
- Am I doing my utmost to make a positive contribution wherever I find myself?

If we can answer yes to the above questions, then there's nothing more we can do. What other people think of us, well, that's their opinion and their business – and it's something we cannot control.

And yes – it's not personal…

The Serenity Prayer

The Serenity Prayer, written by the American theologian Reinhold Niebuhr in 1934, is a brilliant summary of many of the Basic Observations we have just been examining because it's a short, sweet reminder of the fact that there are so many, many things in this Life and in this world which we can do absolutely nothing about. So many, many things which are completely and permanently beyond our control and which we cannot change. I quote his prayer here:

The Serenity Prayer
God grant me the serenity
to accept the things I cannot change;
courage to change the things I can;
and wisdom to know the difference.

Using this prayer on a regular basis is a wonderful way to remind ourselves of the Nature of this thing called Life.

Part 3

Healing Processes

Introduction

Learning to Take Better Care of Ourselves

In Part 1 and Part 2 of this book, we looked at Healthy Models for Relationships and at some of the Basic Observations about the nature of this thing called Life. We looked at the setup of this Life experience – and how we can live more sanely and healthily based on this reality. In other words, healthy living based on the way things really are. Not on the way we would like this Life experience to be, but on the way this Life experience actually is.

Once we begin to understand this information and start to digest it, we can also see that, unfortunately, this information about Healthy Models and the Basic Observations is new to many, if not most, of us. We did not learn about this in school and our parents didn't teach us this information either (mainly because they did not know). As a result, this lack of understanding has often had serious, and sometimes dire consequences on the course of our lives. Unfortunately, our ignorance of the basic mechanisms or principles of this thing called Life is something which affects our behavior, all of our behavior. As a result, we innocently behave in ways which are not conducive to healthy and happy living. For example, we may try to take responsibility for other people or try to "fix" them. Both of which are impossible (see Basic Observations 10 and 8). Or we may become "people-pleasers" or be non-assertive and unable to say "no" and set healthy limits. Or there may be confusion in our relationships when it comes to having healthy boundaries. In short, we are not living in harmony with the Healthy Models described in Part 1 of this book because we are unaware of the Basic Observations outlined in Part 2 of this book. All of which leads to feelings of discomfort and unhappiness in our lives.

In the beginning, when we are young, most of us don't notice this discomfort so much, we just think this is the way things are and get on with it. But sooner or later, when these feelings of discomfort continue long enough, they gain momentum and turn into more and more obvious feelings of distress and unease. And if these feelings of discomfort go on long enough, eventually our bodies start to respond to these negative feelings and emotions, which lead to energy imbalances in our system. Then, sooner or later, these energy imbalances manifest as unpleasant psychological and/or physical symptoms. And finally, when these psychological and/or physical symptoms hang around long enough, we give these symptoms labels or names – and then we have so-called illnesses and "diseases".

Once we begin to understand the information presented in this book as well as the consequences of our lack of understanding of this information, the question then naturally arises: What can we do to correct the energy imbalances and discomfort we have developed as a result of our own ignorance and unhealthy behavior? Is there a way (or methods) to deal with the consequences of all this – and correct the damage? Is it possible? How can we deal with the mental, emotional and physical consequences of not living in harmony with the nature of Life itself?

Part 3 of this book attempts to answer this important question. What to do? How can we deal with the consequences of misaligned energy in our systems and feel better? To achieve this goal, this section will present some simple, practical and highly effective processes you can use to identify, clear up, discharge and heal the consequences and the emotional, psychological and physical damage caused by being unaware of the Healthy Models and Basic Observations described in Parts 1 and 2 of this book.

I suggest you look through the list of the various processes and techniques described in this section, and read and try the ones that seem most suited to your present needs and situation. And then see what happens. Each process listed here is a standalone support process or exercise, so you don't have to read and/or use all of these processes in order to benefit from using any one of them. Just dive in anywhere that appeals to you.

For your information, every single one of the processes presented in this section has been developed as the result of a lifetime of working with clients on just about every issue under the sun. In short, I have used and tested this material, not just on myself, but on countless other individuals.

Does it work?

And one last thing – how will you know if the processes and exercises described here in Part 3 actually work for you? The answer is simple. You will know because you will feel better. That's it. Your feelings, your growing sense of relief and ease will tell you if these exercises are actually working for you. At least that is my experience, both personally and as a person who has worked as a coach and therapist with other people for many, many years. My observation is that, in general, people just feel better when they use the processes and do the exercises described here. (And yes, I have experimented with and worked with these processes and exercises personally for many years.) So the answer is yes, quite simply yes – the techniques, approaches and exercises described in this section of the book do bring relief. But you can only find this out by trying these things out for yourself. So please do!

The Functional Adult and the Wounded Inner Child

The functional adult/wounded inner child model is a very helpful and life-supporting way of framing and understanding our life experiences. So let's look at what I am talking about. For the sake of clarity, it can be very helpful to understand and envision that each one of us actually contains two separate selves. The one self is what I call "the functional adult" and the other is what I call "the wounded inner child". Now what do I mean by this?

The "functional adult" is the grown-up part of you. It's the you who goes to work and pays the bills and goes shopping for food and goes to the movies and takes care of your kids and goes on holiday and does all the many practical things that need doing in your life. In other words, it's the grown-up, educated adult in you. It is the you who is reading this book and who is able to think about things and analyze the concepts, principles and models presented in this book.

And then there is what I call the "wounded inner child". This is the part of you that experienced whatever problems, insecurities, dramas or even traumas that were a part of your early childhood and growing-up years. This is the part of you that is sensitive and probably "wounded" (to some degree) by these early experiences. This description applies to almost everyone because most of us do have some painful memories of painful experiences we had when we were children. And unless these painful experiences have been resolved and healed in some way, they have left their mark on us. In other words, there have been events, people, and situations which have wounded us to some degree. Moreover, the memories of these happenings and events are stored within us as powerful energetic charges or strong feelings and/or even as physical symptoms.

In brief, we can say that the wounded inner child is the repository for all the feelings of discomfort you experienced as a child. The wounds, the pain, the stored energy of any shame or blame or traumas you were subjected to. The feelings of discomfort that arose when you were criticized unjustly or ignored or subjected to unrealistic expectations. The pain you experienced when you were not supported by your family or friends or society for being who you really are. In other words, the feelings and sensations that arose during your childhood (and also thereafter) as a result of the flawed premises that to a large degree run our society today, and which most people are operating on and living by today. Feelings and sensations which probably also were to some degree repressed in order to protect yourself from the discomfort. All of this comprises the wounded inner child.

The interplay of the functional adult and the wounded inner child

So how does this phenomenon or interplay of the functional adult and the wounded inner child play itself out in our daily lives? What is the relationship between these two parts of ourselves? For most average adults who are able to function pretty well in their daily lives, we can say they are mostly operating from the functional adult part of themselves. In other words, it's the functional adult who is (more or less) in control of their lives and activities and who's running the show. And as long as everything is going pretty well and things are pretty much as expected, the wounded inner child part of their personality is lying dormant. In other words, this energy – the wounded inner child energy – is not activated. It's almost as if the wounded inner child is asleep. And so we feel pretty okay. But then, interestingly enough, for most people, there are certain situations or people or events which can really trigger the wounded inner child and awaken this energy. In other words, there can be very specific situations, events or people who can awaken the old pain, the old fears, the old sorrow, the old anger, the old traumas. And when this happens, it can be a pretty upsetting experience. Moreover, if it's a very powerful experience, one can feel as if the functional adult part of oneself has been taken over by this very upset wounded inner child. By a wounded inner child who is flailing about and sometimes even howling.

When this happens, one often has the experience of thinking – wow – what's going on with me? What's happening here? Why am I reacting like this? Why do I feel so upset? This shouldn't be such a big deal, but it is. How come I can't get a handle on what's going on here and just feel normal? Why aren't I my usual self? So yes, that's how it feels. You probably suddenly don't feel like your usual self, which can be a rather unsettling experience. And the reason you don't feel like your normal self is because your wounded inner child has been activated or triggered.

Triggering the wounded inner child

Typical situations where the wounded inner child can be triggered are family get-togethers. Especially if there is tension in the family or a history of problematic relationships. Your life was probably otherwise running smoothly enough, but then suddenly there is a family get-together. It might be a Christmas dinner or birthday party or a trip to the summerhouse where everyone is coming for a summer evening barbecue – and wham bam – what happens? Suddenly your wounded inner child gets triggered. Just seeing all these people – people you have a history with – can be a disconcerting and uncomfortable experience. Which may make you wonder why you are reacting like this. Before you showed up for this event, you felt fine. And even when you thought about the event beforehand while you were at home, you didn't think it would be such a big deal, even if you really don't enjoy so-and-so's company. Regardless, you felt you could easily manage it. But when you actually got there and were confronted with the various people and all their usual idiosyncrasies, you found yourself feeling quite uncomfortable. Because your wounded inner child had been triggered. And powerful emotions arose in you… powerful emotions which can run the gamut from shame and anxiety to irritation and even strong anger.

Other situations which can trigger the wounded inner child can be major life events like divorce, illness, or losing your job. Or they can be less major, daily events like being reprimanded by your boss or having a fight with your partner or getting a speeding ticket. It all depends on your particular background and psychological makeup. Different people have different triggers.

If this rings a bell for you – if you can see and identify that there are situations in your life in which something out of the ordinary is triggered in you, making you feel quite upset and uneasy – this model of the functional adult and the wounded inner child may help you understand and cope better with your experiences.

How to tackle this experience

If this is what you experience from time to time, what can you do about it? Is there a way to cope with situations when you have these kinds of powerful and often unexpected reactions? Is there a way you can function and manage a little more smoothly and comfortably, even when your wounded inner child is awakened?

And the answer is yes. In my experience of working with people for many years, I have discovered that this explanation alone helps so many people understand what's going on with them. Therefore, the first way of dealing with these kinds of situations and your strong reactions is just to remind yourself of this mechanism. To remind yourself and understand that the powerful emotions and sensations you are experiencing are not something you are imagining, but are rather the stored memories, sensations, feelings and energies of events past. And that the present encounter – whatever that happens to be – for some reason has triggered an awakening of this energy which we are now calling the wounded inner child.

Once we can see this and identify this, the next thing that is important to see and understand is that we cannot suppress or make this energy go away – as much as we would like to. Because now it's triggered. And in fact, trying to make this energy go away is equivalent to throwing a wounded little child out on the street because he or she is hurt and is now crying. You know that if you met a little child who was crying and hurt in some way – you would not shame or blame the child or send him or her out on the street in the pouring rain to fend for himself – now would you? No, of course you wouldn't. Well, your own wounded inner child is the same. He or she is a little child who is hurt and upset – and needs your help. Which is why you will only make matters worse by trying to get rid of him or her. You only make matters worse by shaming or blaming yourself for feeling so upset.

So what then? What can you do? Well for starters, instead of shaming and blaming yourself or trying to get rid of your wounded inner child, you can embrace him or her and comfort him or her. In other words, the functional adult part of you, the part of you who is observing what is going on, can take charge of the situation and embrace your own wounded inner child as if you were embracing a wounded little child who came running to you for comfort. Just think about it. What would you do if a little kid had cut his knee and came to you for help and comfort? Well, you would probably embrace the child and take a look at the knee and tell the little boy or girl that it isn't so serious, and then you would wash off the knee and put a bandage on it, and probably say, how about we go and get an ice cream? In other words, you would soothe and comfort this child and make her feel safe. And that's exactly how you should treat your own wounded inner child when he or she is triggered. Soothe and comfort her. Become your own loving and wise parent. Take yourself by the hand and talk to yourself and tell yourself that it's okay to be upset and that you understand exactly why your wounded inner child is upset. Tell him or her that it makes perfect sense that this situation or event or person would upset the child so much. Tell him/her that you understand.

Let the functional adult take charge

Then remind your wounded inner child that you, the grown-up functional adult, are here too. Remind your wounded inner child that you're all grown up now and that you are going to take care of the situation and protect your wounded inner child right now, even if things are a bit challenging. Next remind your inner child that no one is going to mess with you – ever again. Because you're all grown up now. You're not a little child anymore. No, quite the opposite, your grown-up self is here and your grown-up self is wise and strong and resourceful and can handle the situation – even if it seems quite challenging and even if this involves asking other people for help. You can do this – and you will.

This is what dealing with the awakening of your wounded inner child involves. It is all about understanding the mechanism and then meeting yourself with understanding, compassion and love. It's all about understanding that so many of our reactions arise from our previous experiences and the ways in which we have been programmed throughout our life – and especially in our childhood. Moreover, it's important to understand that many of the faulty basic beliefs and programs we learned as children are the basis of these unpleasant and unsettling experiences and behaviors. The unhealthy behavior of our parents, the lack of respect and healthy boundaries, for example, grew out of their own lack of understanding of the Basic Observations about this thing called Life and their ignorance of the Healthy Models for Relationships, which I write about in this book. This is why to clean up what's going on in you – now – it's important to read and contemplate the Healthy Models and Basic Observations described in this book so you get a little more clarity about this thing called Life and understand what you can realistically do something about and what you can't do anything about (like changing other people). And as this new clarity and understanding grows in you, you will find it becomes easier and easier for you to navigate your way through Life and to soothe and comfort your own wounded inner child when he or she gets triggered. Even if this means avoiding certain unhealthy situations (even some family situations) because healthy self-care comes first. That's your job. That's something you can do something about. That's what your functional adult is all about – your right to be you which includes healthy self-care.

Here are some of the things you can do to strengthen the functional adult in you so that you and your functional adult can better soothe, help and comfort the wounded inner child in you.

Read books, go to workshops and/or talk to someone who knows about these things

If you find that the wounded inner child is often triggered in you, I suggest you consciously make up your mind to work on strengthening the functional adult in you. For some people this might include going to a therapist or coach to investigate and better understand the wounds they may be carrying around from their childhood.

In addition, there are many good books and workshops that

deal with healing the wounded inner child and strengthening the functional adult side of you. John Bradshaw's book *Homecoming – Reclaiming and Championing Your Inner Child* is a good support as are many of the 12-Step Programs such as ACA. I also highly recommend the books of Pia Mellody (see Recommended Reading at the end of this book).

Strengthening the functional adult

Another good way you can strengthen the functional adult in you and support your wounded inner child is to make a list of your adult strengths and your resources.

Here's what to do: Get out a piece of paper and write down all the things you have done and can do that demonstrate to yourself that you are all grown-up now and can take care of yourself. Start with easy stuff like you went to school and have an education, and that today you have a job or will soon have one. You are making your own money and you're actually good at what you do. You can walk, talk, work, you're intelligent, you can read and write and understand and explain things… in other words take a good look at the fact that you're not a little kid anymore. Write down and notice and let your own wounded inner child see and understand clearly that you really are all grown-up now and can take care of yourself.

Next you can add to your list all the things you can think of that you are really good at. Like for example, you're good with your hands and at fixing stuff, or you're a good cook, or you're good with computers, or you're a good mother, or you're good at painting or singing or running or of taking care of children or at gardening. Notice all this stuff too and write it down on your list. These are the things that characterize you and make you a strong, independent and interesting person.

You can also write down all your work qualifications, your expertise, your education and what you are working on and studying right now. Plus what about what you are working towards? Do you have specific career goals or are you set on buying an old house and renovating it or is it your dream to start your own business?

Then start writing down your emotional characteristics and strengths. What qualities characterize you? Are you empathic? Do you have a sense of humor? Are you fun to be with? Are you reliable? Are you hard-working and loyal? Are you good at socializing? Are you creative? Are you a visionary? Write down whatever characterizes you and makes you, you!

Once you've made your list, look at your list every day. And keep adding to it as you think of and remember other strengths and qualities that demonstrate that you are all grown-up now and can take care of yourself. Once you begin to get a handle on this, you will see how much this exercise helps when your wounded inner child gets triggered. First, because the wounded inner child feels safer when there is a functional adult around to take care of things. And secondly because your wounded inner child also understands that you – the functional adult part of you – can meet the scared and hurt little child in you with understanding thanks to all of the strengths and resources you possess today as a functional adult. All of this makes your wounded inner child feel safe – and then, when your wounded inner child feels safer, he/she will begin to relax. And then guess what happens – you will feel better too!

For more good exercises to strengthen the functional adult in you, see Healing Process No. 7: *Using the Power of Mind Wisely for Healing and Recovery.*

Using the power of your mind to strengthen the functional adult

It also helps to strengthen the functional adult in you to understand and learn to use the power of your mind more wisely. This is one of your greatest resources – your ability to understand the way your mind works and to use your mind to strengthen the wise, functional adult in you. I know you have this ability because one of the Laws of the Universe says that *whatever we focus our attention on grows in our experience.* This is the amazing power of our minds and this powerful law is our key to harnessing the power of our minds to improve our lives.

For more details about this mechanism, see Healing Process No. 7: *Using the Power of Mind Wisely for Healing and Recovery* and Healing Process No. 8: *The Great Universal Intelligence – the Greatest Healing Power of All.* The information and exercises provided in those chapters will help you in various ways to strengthen and stabilize your functional adult. (We can also say all the information provided in this book helps strengthen the functional adult in each one of us!)

Working with your inner child

Once you are feeling a little more stable in your functional adult and know you can meet and embrace your inner child with understanding and love, you can begin to work consciously to get in touch with him or her and have a talk. There are several ways to do this:

The first thing you can do is to just sit in a chair or on your bed and imagine that this little child (you) is sitting right next to you. Then put your arm around your inner child and envision yourself talking to him/her. And then listen to what your inner child has to say to you.

If this seems too abstract, the following left hand/right hand writing exercise usually works for everyone. Here's what to do. Sit down and take out a piece of paper (or write in your journal) and then write with your right hand (if you are right-handed) or with your left hand (if you are left-handed). This is your functional adult who is writing and you are going to write to your inner child as follows:

Dear Little _____ (your name),
How are you?
Love,
Big _____ (your name)

Then you switch the pen to the other hand because now it is your inner child who is going to write and answer your functional adult. So now you use your left hand (if you are right-handed) or your right hand (if you are left-handed). So now, your inner child writes back using your untrained hand and answers:

Dear Big _____ (your name)
I am scared... (or whatever your inner child wants to reply)
Little _____ (your name)

You will discover that using your untrained hand to write is difficult to do and this helps you get in touch with your inner child.

Once your inner child has answered, switch hands again because now it's time for your functional adult to reply to what your inner child has said. This time when you reply, remember it is the job of your functional adult to help make your inner child feel safe. So don't make your inner child wrong and don't try to fix your inner child. Just listen to what her or she has said and then meet him/her where he/she is. Tell your inner child that you are there and that you are always going to be there and never leave your inner child. So you can write, for example:

Dear Little _____ (your name)
It's okay to be afraid. I understand. But I'm here and I'm going to take care of you and I'm never going to leave you. What are you afraid of?
Love,
Big _____ (your name)

Then switch hands again and see what your inner child answers. Keep writing back and forth until you feel you've done enough. Then let it rest. Try again the next day or whenever you have time. And watch what happens in your life as a result of this exercise. Most people I've worked with get amazing insights into themselves from writing to their inner child like this.

Emotional Decompression

Another good tool for meeting and dealing with the energy of your wounded inner child is Emotional Decompression. This is a powerful exercise which anyone can use to locate, decompress and release this old energy and the pent-up feelings that are trapped and stored inside of us and which become activated when the wounded inner child is triggered. For a detailed description of how to do Emotional Decompression, see Healing Process No. 4.

In conclusion

Now to summarize this chapter: As you begin to understand the mechanism of the functional adult and the wounded inner child in yourself, you will discover that you can better understand what happens in your life when your wounded inner child is triggered or activated. Once you start working with this concept and are more aware of this mechanism, you will then be better able to cope with and meet situations where you get triggered with understanding. Moreover, you will find that not only can you identify what triggers you, you will even learn that you can actually prepare yourself for situations where you know in advance you will probably be triggered. You will be better prepared and no longer surprised at what happens inside of you. Which means you will now know how to take better care of your wounded inner child, even if she/he gets scared and unhappy. You will recognize what's going on and as a result you will also now know that the functional adult in you can take control of the situation and manage, even if you do feel challenged for a while.

Healing Process No. 2

Dealing With Stress

Stress is a really big issue in today's busy world and the word "stress" is often being used as a sort of universal "catch-all" or label for just about anything and everything that may ail anyone. We often hear that someone is "down with stress" and I coach people every day who are on sick leave because of stress. So let's try to slow things down just a little bit and look at the Nature of this thing called Life and what any one single individual might be able to realistically do in relation to feeling and experiencing "stress".

Stress is a purely subjective experience

So what is stress? The dictionary says stress is: "a state of mental or emotional strain or tension resulting from adverse or very demanding circumstances". But who gets to define what is "adverse or very demanding"? If we look carefully, we will discover that what is adverse or demanding to one person is not necessarily adverse or demanding to another. So "demanding" according to whom? When we understand the Basic Observations described in Part 2 of this book, we also understand that stress has to be a purely subjective experience, because everything in our Life is a purely subjective experience. This means that stress, like everything else, all depends on who the person is, and how this person interprets and thus experiences the events, situations or tasks at hand. Consequently, we come to understand that what is stressful to one person is not necessarily stressful to another. It all depends on who the person is and on the many factors involved, and how the person interprets them and the situation.

If this is true, how then can we more realistically define

stress? I would suggest that the feeling of *stress arises when there is a perceived imbalance between the task or situation at hand and the perceived resources of the person involved in the situation. In other words, when a person feels overwhelmed because he or she feels or believes he or she does not have the resources required to deal with the task or situation at hand, then the person experiences so-called "stress".*

There can be many reasons why a person may feel overwhelmed. For example, the person can perceive or feel or experience that there is a lack of:

- time
- expertise (skills, knowledge, understanding)
- money
- energy, strength or health
- help or assistance
- support and/or understanding from the other people involved in the situation
- clarity about what the task is about or requires, who does what, when
- etc.

And this perceived lack is always in relation to the task or the perceived demands of the task or situation at hand. Thus we can see that stress is a subjective and relational experience. There is a perceived imbalance between the stressed person's assessment of their own abilities in relation to the perceived requirements of a situation or task. Accordingly, if this is the case, what can a person who is feeling stressed actually do? There are two ways of evaluating this situation and making appropriate adjustments. We can look at the person's internal state and then we can look at the external situation.

The person's internal state

Let's start by looking at the person's internal state. By this I mean, let's look at the way in which the person assesses the situation. First and foremost, if you are stressed, it's important to have a more realistic assessment of the situation you are in – and of life in general. So start with the basic, general understanding which applies to everything in life – and that is – there is no ideal or "perfect solution" or perfect answer to any situation or to the task at hand. Every situation and every task is always made up of a multitude of factors, most of which are beyond your control. But right now, you are faced with the present situation, and if you are realistic, you will be able to assess, more or less realistically, what you can hope to accomplish. This has nothing to do with achieving a "perfect solution", since no such thing exists.

So first and foremost, stop making the situation or task into an "either/or" scenario in your mind. Stop thinking that either you're a total success and can "fix" or "deal" with everything or else you are a total fiasco and failure and can do nothing. It's never like that. It's never so black and white or "either/or". Reality is always much more nuanced and much more moderate.

If you are reasonably realistic you can probably figure out what you can actually sensibly do and accomplish. Once you have figured that out, once you have made a more realistic assessment of what you can actually do in the present situation – then stick to that. In other words – moderation! *Moderation!* Take the middle road. Do the best you can and forget the rest. This can be a really difficult state of mind to achieve, especially if you are a perfectionist! Perfectionism is the cause of so much stress and suffering – and why? Because perfectionism goes against reality. And because, as I said above, there is no "perfect" way to do things, no "perfect" solution. No final, definitive answer, no "this is it" solution – now and forever. The reality is that things keep evolving and changing, and if you want to experience less stress, it's a good idea to be realistic about this. And this doesn't mean you shouldn't give it your best shot. Of course, you can and should. But when you've done that, well then, let it go!

And then go for a walk in the park! Or take a break! Or kick off your shoes and watch a movie. Or go for a run or go to a cafe and drink a cup of coffee and stare blankly into space for a while. But regardless, give yourself a break! (For more about moderation, see Healthy Model No. 16.)

All of the above is what I would call "sane self-talk". It amounts to you talking sanely and maturely to yourself. And when this happens, who's doing the talking here? It's the "functional adult" in you, the grown-up you who is wise and strong and who can take charge of a situation like this in a grown-up and psychologically mature manner. That's who's talking. Because the reality is, when we're overwhelmed and stressed, it's often the "wounded inner child" part of us that has been triggered by the situation. For more insight into this mechanism of what happens when our wounded inner child gets triggered, see the previous Healing Process No. 1 about *The Functional Adult and the Wounded Inner Child*.

But back to what the functional adult in you can realistically do after you've taken a deep breath and gone for a walk in the nearest park.

Realistic planning and time management

Here are some of the things we can do starting with the matter of realistic planning and time management. So let's slow everything down and look at the various aspects of good planning and time management.

1) Everything takes longer than you think
The first rule of realistic planning is to understand that everything – and I mean everything – always takes at least 15-

20% longer (and sometimes even longer) than you expect it will take. Everything. And this goes for everyone. So please factor this in on your daily "to do" list. Then try to be more realistic about what you can actually accomplish in a day.

2) Prioritize

Next: prioritize! What's really important here? What's in the "need to do" category and what's in the "nice to do" category? Making lists where you divide the things you believe you have to do into a "need to do" and a "nice to do" category can be very helpful. In fact, many people feel an immediate sense of relief when they realize there isn't so much to do on their "need to do" list... that so much of what they are worried about is actually about things on their "nice to do" list. In other words, stuff which is not so important as they thought it was. So please give this a try. And really ask yourself if each specific task is a "need to do" activity or a "nice to do" activity. Be really clear about this. Then focus, first and foremost, on the "need to do" stuff.

You can also prioritize the various tasks on your "need to do" list. Which ones are the most important, the most pressing? Which ones can wait a bit? How much time will each task realistically take? Is the time frame or deadline for each task realistic or do you need more time?

When I coach people and we do these lists together, almost everyone tells me they experience an immediate sense of relief by categorizing their tasks in this way. Once they've got their "need to do" list written down clearly, they usually sail out of my office with big smiles on their faces.

3) One day at a time

Next rule in better time management is to "take one day at a time". Nothing is more stressful, especially in a big project, than getting too far ahead into the future in your mind. Why?

Because when you do this, it almost always creates a sense of overwhelm because then the task seems so big and complex. But if you take one day at a time – and break the day into bit-size bits and tasks – it makes everything feel much more doable. In other words, say to yourself – today I'm going to do this – and then keep your focus on that instead of all the time stressing yourself by worrying about getting to your final result. If you focus on "one day at a time", it makes it so much easier to get where you want to go.

4) Ask for help and delegate

Next – ask for help. Remember, whether we are talking about the workplace or the home front, your colleagues and family are not mind readers. Other people do not know what you are up against or what you are dealing with if you don't tell them. (Remember Basic Observation 7 that we can't get inside other people's heads and that other people can't get inside our heads.) So tell people what's going on – and don't expect them to just figure things out for themselves. Let them know what the situation is and then ask for the necessary assistance, support, expertise, time – whatever it is you need to manage the situation in a more realistic way.

5) Setting limits

And finally, there is the setting limits and having healthy boundaries for oneself. In order to do something like this, each one of us has to get to know who we are in a more honest and realistic way and begin to honestly define one's own limits. This is often something which many people may not actually ever have done before because they were never in a situation where they felt so much pressure. So let's be clear about this. Defining one's limits for oneself can be very anxiety-provoking, especially if you're a people-pleaser and are worried about or afraid (or terrified) of incurring other people's disapproval.

Because what if your limits don't please everyone!

But as difficult and anxiety-provoking as this idea may be to many of us, it's one of the big issues that the whole matter of stress brings up in people. Because you have to ask yourself questions like:

- How far am I willing to go?
- How much discomfort can I actually handle?
- Is it worth the price?
- What are the alternatives?
- What would happen if I just said "no"?
- Who am I really?
- What's my life all about?
- Why am I really doing this?
- Is this really how I want to live?
- What do I really want to do with my life?
- Are there other options?

So yes, suffering from stress often sets off an avalanche of internal questions... which is a good thing because the pain can be so acute that it forces people to ask themselves the really big questions. To really ask themselves what life is really all about and who they are and how they really want to spend their precious life energy.

But back to what to do. Once you have defined yourself and your limits a little more clearly and realistically, the next step is then to figure out how to communicate this information clearly and skillfully to the other people involved in the situation. Which leads us to the next section – how to deal with the external situation.

The external situation

When all the above is said and done, there is also the question of the expectations of the various people in each concrete situation.

For example, what are the expectations of the workplace or the family to the person who is experiencing stress? Are the expectations of the person's surroundings reasonable and realistic? Are these expectations fair and respectful or does the workplace or the family have unrealistic expectations or demands to you as an employee on the job or family member? (You have an Inner Compass so how do you feel about this? See Healthy Model No. 7 for more about this mechanism.) Consequently, what can you do if you've tried to look at the situation as realistically as you can and you perceive that the expectations or demands from the people involved are unrealistic, unreasonable or disrespectful? What can you do about that?

First of all, you can talk to your workplace and the people involved and/or to your family members about the situation. Because the reality may well be that the workplace or family does have unrealistic expectations or demands to your skill, energy, ability, or expertise – or to what the project or task actually requires. It may also be the case that the other people involved are unaware of what the situation actually is and what the task or project at hand requires. Therefore, this information should be conveyed as clearly and skillfully as possible to the people involved. Let them know what's going on and how you feel about it. See the section about assertiveness and clear communications (Healthy Model No. 8) and the section about healthy boundaries (Healthy Model No. 9).

If, however, your attempts at clear communications and setting healthy boundaries fall on deaf ears, remember that in the final analysis, you can always say "no". Regardless of how provocative this thought may seem at first, it is always possible to say "no". (And yes, everything we say and do has consequences. See Healthy Model No. 15 for more about this.) But remember, not only is it possible to say "no", it is your right and privilege as a free human being to know where your limits are and to clearly define what you are willing to be a part of – and what you are not willing to be a part of. Understanding and manifesting these limits is also called "integrity". In this connection, if you are having difficulty saying "no", it is a good idea to ask yourself why you feel you have to live up to other people's expectations to you. Why? What is this about? How did you learn to be such a people-pleaser? Read the Basic Observations in Part 2 of this book again until you begin to understand that it is impossible to please everyone, no matter how hard you try because you cannot get into other people's heads and control their thoughts and feelings.

Healthy self-care

Finally, remember that you have to take care of yourself first. This is not as selfish as it may seem at first glance, but rather just common sense. Healthy self-care is a prerequisite to doing anything of value for anyone at any time. Whether it's being an effective employee, a supportive colleague or fair boss, a good partner or a good parent. Because if you yourself are stressed out of your mind and on the verge of collapse, it is almost impossible to be of value or assistance to anyone else. So remind yourself often that when you feel good and have good energy, your ability to do good work and help other people or be a positive influence at your job or in your family increases greatly.

The importance of healthy self-care is a little like flying in an airplane with small children. I have three sons so I remember how it was when I flew with them when they were small. The stewardess explained that if the pressure in the cabin dropped and the oxygen masks came down over our heads, it was important for me (the mother) to put my own mask on first – before I helped my children. This is because if a mother puts the masks on her children first and then blacks out or drops dead from lack of oxygen – how can she help them? So we're talking about the same principle here. Help yourself first, so you can help others. Take good care of yourself first, so you can live up to your own aspirations of being a good employee, good leader, good partner or good parent. Your ability to be of benefit to your workplace, family or society in general is always in direct proportion to how good your own energy is. To how strong and healthy you are and how on target you are feeling about life and your life situation.

Healing Process No. 3

Truth Telling

It's hard to make any real progress on the journey of self-discovery, self-realization, self-empowerment and healing without telling the truth. We have to tell the truth to understand what's going on with us. We have to tell the truth to get the energy moving. We have to tell the truth for change to happen in our lives. The truth about what? The truth about everything. We have to tell the truth about Life and how we experience it. We have to tell the truth about how we feel. We have to tell the truth about ourselves, about the people we know, about our families, about the situations we've been in, about what has happened to us – and about what we have experienced and what we've been through. We can only be ourselves by doing this – by telling the truth. If we don't tell the truth, who are we? And when we do tell the truth, we also find out who we are. Interestingly enough, when this happens – when we tell the truth and are ourselves, we also set ourselves free. Nothing is more liberating than telling the truth.

Until this happens, until we tell the truth, we often remain stuck in our old patterns, programs and belief systems. Our old conditioned responses and habitual reactions just continue. In many cases, these old habits and patterns actually grow stronger because our old patterns of thinking and behaving just gain more and more momentum. So until we begin telling the truth, we often find ourselves stuck in a rut. But the moment we begin telling the truth, the magic of change can begin.

Truth telling is obviously a very well-known, effective therapeutic tool that has been used by psychologists, psychiatrists, psychoanalysts, therapists, coaches, counselors, self-help groups, 12-Step Programs and more, for many, many years. But even though this is the case – and even though many people today know about or have heard about the benefits of truth telling – it can still be very beneficial for us to look at what exactly truth telling is all about – and how to do it.

Tell what happened to you

Firstly, truth telling is telling what you have experienced. In other words, what happened and how you experienced it and how you felt about it and how you feel about it today. It's all about you. It's not about what other people think happened. It's not about what your mother or father thought or think happened. It's not about what your partner thinks happened or what your children think happened. It's just about you. What you think happened. Your experience. That's it.

It's also not about what you think you "should" think and feel. It's about what you actually do think and feel. It's about getting in touch with yourself. With your life experience. With what you know to be true for you. Without censoring it or modifying it or editing it. But obviously, this is not an easy thing to do for any of us. For several reasons:

First of all because so many of us are afraid of the consequences and of what will happen if we actually do tell the truth. That is why I always say to clients when we're doing truth telling in my office, let's just forget about the consequences for now. Let's make the decision that you are going to tell the truth and that you don't have to act on what you are discovering and saying (not now and not ever) if you don't want to. Just tell me the truth. Just say it for you. You don't have to tell another soul. Just start by telling me (your coach/therapist). Your truth is safe with me, I am never going to tell another soul (unless of course you tell me you murdered someone).

I also always say to people that once they've told the truth, if they do want to do something about it and say something to other people, well, then we come to the matter of what I call "constructive communications". In other words, how to communicate respectfully and skillfully with the people you may have issues with. But that is a whole other project. For now, let's just leave worrying about what to do with this information aside and focus on doing truth telling.

The second reason why we're not used to telling the truth is because we've been programmed from an early age to believe there is a right and wrong way to think and feel. Moreover, most of us have also been programmed to please others. This is why it can be quite challenging and even anxiety-provoking to get in touch with what you really and truly think and feel. And then – on top of that – to actually say it out loud to another person. Wow. Now that often takes great courage.

But it's a good thing to do. It really is. Because – as anyone who has tried it will tell you – you just feel better when you tell the truth about how you feel. You just feel lighter, more enlightened, and relieved. And you feel more clarity about who you are and what you've experienced. That's just the way it is. And when you feel better, relieved, lighter, you just know for yourself that truth telling actually works.

This is what truth-telling is all about in its most basic form.

Telling the truth to another person

There are different ways one can tell the truth. Let's start with telling the truth to another person. In practice, it's often easiest and best to go to a professional therapist, psychologist, psychotherapist or coach and tell the truth to this person. Because this person is trained to listen and acknowledge you and probably has some understanding of the challenges we human beings face in our daily lives. Sessions with a trusted therapist can truly be life-changing and liberating. But it's a good idea to realize that this can also often be challenging and it might take a while to get into the flow of actually talking honestly to another person. But I highly recommend you give it a try and see what happens. It is also important to be aware that if the chemistry is not good between you and this person, you should go to someone else. You have an Inner Compass and if you do not feel comfortable with this person, go somewhere else. And don't be afraid to try several people until you find someone you feel safe and comfortable with. Again this is about learning to trust your truth.

And what about talking to friends? Most of us do this to begin with, but I often warn my own clients about being realistic when it comes to talking to their friends about their issues. The problem with talking to friends is that even though your friends care for you and want to support you and really do wish you well, your friends are usually not trained to listen and encourage you to find your own truth. Most often your friends will have their own ideas about what is best for you – so listening to friends can often make people feel even more confused. I hear this all the time from my clients. This is why I often suggest to clients to take a break from discussing their issues with their friends, at least while they are working with me. And until they get a little more clarity about who they really are and feel a little more stable, in terms of who they are and in terms of acknowledging their own truth. This is also why I've written a whole book – called *Find and Follow Your Inner Compass* – which is all about learning to trust and follow your own internal guidance system, if you want to live more happily and be more in alignment with your own truth. It's also good to remember that the sign of a good coach or therapist is that this person will almost never tell you what to do but will encourage you to find your own answers.

Writing the truth

Writing things down is another good way to practice truth telling. You can write about a specific incident or experience you've had, either something recent or something that happened in the distant past. It doesn't matter. Just do this for your own sake. Just do this to tell your own truth. You could write about the breakup of a relationship or about an argument or a situation at work or about some misunderstanding with a family member. Try picking something very concrete and specific, and write about what happened and how you experienced this situation and this person. Writing these things down is much more revealing and liberating than we often think it will be. The important thing is to let yourself go – don't try to be calm or censor yourself or think you have to justify everything you think and feel. Just write down what you are really feeling and see what happens. You don't have to show this to anyone. This is just for you. And remember if you tell yourself the truth about how you feel, it doesn't mean you have to act on it. Another way to practice telling the truth is by writing a letter to someone. If you are sad or hurt or upset or angry about something that happened with another person (be it someone close or even just an acquaintance), you can write to the person and honestly say what you are thinking and feeling. It can be a wonderful exercise, especially if you decide from the very beginning that you don't actually have to send your letter to this person. Knowing that you don't actually have to send your letter will free you up enough so you can just write down the truth and tell what you are actually feeling for your own sake. So start by writing this letter for your own sake. To tell your own truth so you can read the letter and so that you can hear it for yourself. This is a very good way to begin truth telling. Just do it for you. Just do it to tell and to hear your own truth.

You can always decide later if you actually want to send your letter to this person. And if you do, this is where constructive communication comes into the picture. If you do want to send your letter, do you really want to send this raw, uncut version or should you try to formulate your truth in a more diplomatic and skillful way? Read Healthy Model No. 5: *It's Not What You Say –*

But How You Say It for input and ideas about how to formulate your communications in a more constructive and skillful way.

But back to truth telling. As I said from the beginning, it takes some practice for most of us to, first of all, get in touch with what we actually think and feel about difficult situations or people in our lives, and then secondly to actually write it down. But it's definitely worth the effort because it can be such a revealing, enlightening and liberating experience.

And finally, it's important to remember that strong emotions may come up when you are writing your own truth. So it's important to understand that this is part of the process of telling the truth and that it's important to just allow and accept how you feel. Even if you get angry or want to cry or feel like stomping and stamping around the room. Just allow and accept whatever comes up to come up. For more about how to deal with powerful emotions arising, see the next Healing Process No. 4 on *Emotional Decompression*.

Truth telling for people who are more seriously challenged

If you are more seriously challenged or have serious issues (or if you are a therapist who is working with someone who is more seriously challenged), the first prerequisite for truth telling to someone else is the establishment of a feeling of trust and safety between you, the person who is seeking help, and the therapist. In order to be honest, you should feel, at the very minimum, a basic sense of safety in the therapist's presence. Moreover, you should hopefully feel that the therapist is there for you and respects you, regardless of what your story is. (This is especially important for people who have experienced some kind of trauma. In cases like this, the need for safety and respect is paramount.) Now to the actual truth telling itself. Whatever it is you are asked about or want to talk about, it's important to understand that this is a process and that this can take time. Which means to begin with, just identifying what you want to talk about and then slowly telling what happened to you... and then eventually sharing these experiences in as much detail as possible. Often in the beginning, when people are asked about something difficult or traumatic, they may say, "Oh I can't remember that." Or, "I don't remember exactly what happened." Or, "It's just one big blank." But this is almost never the case – regardless of how repressed or suppressed a memory may be, it is there. But people often do not have immediate access to the information (especially if it is traumatic). But it is stored somewhere anyway. And by talking slowly and in detail about whatever little bits and pieces of information a person can remember, most people will slowly gain access to more and more information. Sometimes this happens very slowly and sometimes memories just come flooding back; it depends on who you are and on a multitude of factors including what the issue is/was and how long ago it happened or began. But, in general, by delving slowly into details like, where were you, what were you wearing, what season of the year was it, who else was there, whatever you can remember... all these little bits of information will often help jog a person's ability to access more and more information. So it's an excellent strategy to go slowly in order to connect to more and more details.

I often say it's like you have a very tightly-packed little suitcase that has been closed and locked for years and years. And now we're going to open it. At first when we open it, it's just a jumble of tightly-packed old stuff that you don't recognize or understand. But if you unpack the suitcase very slowly and carefully, picking up one little item at a time, and unfold it slowly, you will most likely be very surprised at what you discover. So take each item out of your little suitcase carefully and look at it slowly and consider it carefully from all sides. And again, this doesn't have to be done in one or two or three sessions; in fact it's probably better that it takes many sessions to look at and unpack the same event until you (or the person you are working with) reaches a point where some kind of clarity emerges for the person who is telling the truth.

A good therapist will probably ask questions like: "How did it feel?" Or, "How did you feel about it at the time?" Or, "How do you feel about it now?" And why? What was going on? What made you angry? Or sad? Or upset? Or frustrated? Or afraid?

The key here is always to allow whatever comes up to come up – and to then just acknowledge whatever actually does come up.

It is also important to understand that when you are telling the truth, powerful feelings and emotions can and do come up. When this happens, it is absolutely crucial to understand the importance of this and to understand that you must try to accept and allow these feelings to emerge – as much as possible. A good therapist will always help you to understand that you shouldn't try to suppress these feelings or shut them down again, because that's probably what you have been doing most of your life. Therefore, when telling the truth, it's time for the opposite to happen. It's time to allow feelings to surface and emerge. And it's important to understand that these feelings are not dangerous. So the good therapist will most likely explain, over and over again, that yes, feelings can be very powerful and often unpleasant, but they are not dangerous. They are just old, suppressed energy.

Allowing and accepting feelings

So yes, feelings are just energy. And this energy can be unpleasant but it is not dangerous. Because the truth about feelings is the more we try to suppress them, the more powerful they become. But when we allow and accept this energy and our feelings, they arise, and maybe hang around for a little while, and then the energy and the feelings just dissipate and disappear. Which is why the very best way to meet feelings is to "allow and accept" them. Just let them come up. Just sit with them. And allow the energy to dissipate. And remember there is *no healing without feeling*.

This is the key here. To keep reminding ourselves – when unpleasant emotions arise – that by resisting them and fighting against them (or trying to keep them locked away), the only thing that happens is that they gain energy and become more and more powerful. This is so important to understand – that by resisting them we are actually giving more energy to these feelings. Which makes them seem more powerful. And when this happens, we may then become afraid because we fear that these emotions will be so powerful that they will overwhelm us. Or we won't be able to handle them. But the reverse is actually true. By allowing and accepting our feelings and emotions – regardless of how powerful they may seem in the moment – what really happens is they arise and dissipate and disappear by themselves. This is big news for most of us because so many of us have been programmed to fear our emotions. But when we learn to allow and accept our emotions, then the magic of healing can begin. Perhaps only slowly at first, but little by little, healing definitely begins.

But it is important to understand, this almost never happens all at once or only once. Working with feelings – allowing and accepting them – is an ongoing process. That is why it is important to understand that feelings arise like waves on the ocean. They come and go and sometimes there are powerful waves. A really big wave may sweep over you but then it will pass and things will calm down again... and then another wave will probably come...

So again, the trick here is to allow and accept. Just allow and accept. Let the feelings come – like waves coming into the shore. Just allow them to arise – whatever they are. And keep reminding yourself over and over again that there can be *no healing without feeling*. And understand that it's not enough to just be mental and think and talk about what has happened. The process only works when we allow ourselves to actually "feel" how we felt – whether it's grief, anger, rage, sadness, heartbreak, fear... whatever it is... just accept and allow these feelings to be there. (For more about how to process your emotions as they come up, see the next Healing Process No. 4: *Emotional Decompression.*)

Truth telling for people who are traumatized: Transforming trauma into personal power

In the case of serious trauma, I highly recommend seeking the help of highly trained therapists or professionals who are familiar with trauma and who are used to working with people who have been traumatized. By serious trauma, I mean abuse such as rape, incest and other types of violence or war experiences. In addition, coming from a seriously dysfunctional family, especially when there is psychological abuse and/or alcohol or physical abuse, also falls into this category. All of these types of trauma may result in various long-term psychological problems including PTSD (Post Traumatic Stress Disorder).

In addition to all the guidelines I outlined above – including the importance of establishing a sense of trust and safety with a therapist – it is also very important for the person who has had these traumatic experiences to be able to acknowledge that they have been violated. To acknowledge that "wrong-doing" or "evil" or "injustice" has occurred. That this action or activity (whatever it was) was not okay but rather a violation of our basic human rights. And that it was a very traumatic experience. In these situations, the therapist is the "witness" who acknowledges to, for, and with the person that "evil" or "injustice" has been done. This is a very important part of the healing process. That wrong-doing is acknowledged and witnessed.

In connection with this, it is important not only to

acknowledge that "wrong-doing" has occurred but also that the person has the right to grieve for the loss he or she has suffered. The loss of innocence, the loss of trust, whatever the loss is... And moreover, the fact that this "wrong-doing" cannot be undone or changed. That it did happen and it happened to this person. We are talking about acknowledging the wound, the violence, the suffering, the abandonment that a fellow human being has experienced. And allowing this person to feel all the grief, rage, sorrow, anger and loss involved. This is what the process is all about. This is what healing is all about.

We can also call the anger experienced in these types of situations "righteous anger". I am talking about the anger which arises when someone has suffered grievous harm, violence or injustice. (For more about this healthy anger, see Healthy Model No. 11 about *The Difference Between Anger and Personal Power*.) In this connection, it is important to understand that this righteous anger can be a wonderful source of healing and of energy which can be channeled into future social action.

For many people, righteous anger can be channeled into and used as a force for good in the world. This is what transforming trauma into personal power is all about. That a person's life experience becomes a very powerful force for good in the world and a very powerful force for change. Many people who are today powerful and effective advocates for social change, truth and social justice have themselves suffered grievous harm. But they have used their own traumatic experiences and what they have learned as a force for good. As a result, they have dedicated themselves to working with others for change and to prevent more injustice. People like this may become teachers or activists or other types of change agents – teaching and working for social justice as well as trying to bring the perpetrators of these heinous crimes to justice.

In this way, those who have been wounded, and are still wounded, may be able to transform their own traumatic experiences into a powerful force for good in the world. They have transformed trauma into personal power, which they then go on to use to support others who have also been traumatized. You will find people motivated by righteous anger everywhere, working with support groups, or becoming therapists, counselors, teachers or coaches themselves or through writing or by becoming social activists.

> *"When I despair, I remember that all through history the way of truth and love has always won. There have been tyrants and murderers, and for a time they can seem invincible, but in the end they always fall. Think of it. Always."* Gandhi

The healing process of truth telling when abuse has occurred (in brief)

In brief, the healing process of truth telling for people who have suffered abuse can be seen to have 3 main phases or stopping points along the way:

Stage 1
    Recognizing what happened
    Starting to tell the truth
    Coming out of denial about what happened to one

Stage 2 (the re-active stage)
    Continuing to come out of denial
    Really telling the truth about the lies
        Breaking the insidious code of silence in many families
        and relationships
    Initiating healthy self-care
    Taking measures for healthy self-defense
        Staying away from abusive people (even if, for example,

it happens to be a family member(s) or a former partner)
Setting healthy boundaries
Not seeing the abuser(s) anymore
Not interacting with them
Leaving abusive relationships (if it's a partner or family members)

Stage 3 (the pro-active stage)
Coming back for justice
Really coming out of denial
Telling the truth about the lies
Telling the truth about the lies to others and the world
Seeking justice legally when possible
Asking for apologies and for people to make amends
Helping others in similar situations do the same
Becoming an advocate for justice wherever one is in his or her life journey and in whatever ways feel appropriate

One final word: Encountering and clearing up flawed premises during truth telling

It is important to add here that during the process of attempting to tell the truth – regardless of whether we are talking about so-called "ordinary people" with "ordinary, everyday problems" or people who are more seriously challenged – almost everyone discovers and encounters many of the flawed premises about life that they believed in, or still believe in, which have probably prevented them from being able to tell the truth from the very beginning. In other words, we discover the beliefs and flawed premises that are keeping us shut down and in lockdown. We discover the faulty collective beliefs and/or family beliefs that have nothing to do with the Nature of this thing called Life. We discover beliefs such as what I call the "myth of family" which says that family is more important than anything else. More important than treating our fellow human beings with kindness and respect. This is a myth or collective belief which blocks many people from telling the truth about the abuse they have suffered, or are suffering, in their families and relationships. Or we may discover beliefs about being responsible for the happiness of other people, which can prevent us from telling the truth about the behavior of other people in our life and relationships. The list is long indeed of the flawed premises and faulty beliefs that can block our ability to tell the truth.

So in this way, the Healthy Models for Relationships in Part 1 of this book as well as the Basic Observations about the setup here in this Life experience, described in Part 2, will be valuable tools and insights which can help people identify and free themselves from the many flawed premises and faulty beliefs which may be blocking people's ability to access and tell the truth about what has happened to them.

Healing Process No. 4

Emotional Decompression

In our work with healing and recovery, the question inevitably arises – what can we do with the powerful, and often unpleasant, emotions that we feel? Emotional decompression is a powerful and effective tool that can help us in the process of healing and recovery, whether it is our own process or we are working to guide and help others. To begin, let's start by defining what we are talking about.

The difference between our thinking and our feelings

It is important to understand that there is a difference between what we think, in other words, our mental understanding of events and the actual physical energy of our feelings. Because feelings are energetic impulses which we experience depending on our interpretation of what is happening to us. The interesting thing here is to understand that these feelings (whatever they are) are stored in our physical bodies as energetic or somatic memories. In other words, each somatic memory we have is linked to various events and emotions which many of us have most likely suppressed – or at least have very little connection to or contact with.

But if we look closely, we will find that our physical bodies remember everything that has ever happened to us. It's all recorded there because every memory has a physical memory track. It's really fascinating to discover this. And interesting to think about and understand because this can open the doors to new and radical ways of healing physical and emotional distress. Moreover, it also leads us to the amazing insight that physical and emotional distress (in the final analysis) are actually one and the same thing.

Just think about it. What are all our physical sensations about anyway? What are they telling us? After all, the body doesn't lie. And if the body doesn't lie, what is it telling us? Especially if we can, at least theoretically, accept the premise that everything that has happened to us is recorded in our bodies, then what are all these sensations telling us?

It's a fascinating experiment and definitely worth exploring.

A closer look at emotional and physical discomfort

Let's start by taking a closer look at our emotions, which are the signals we are receiving from within ourselves. Our emotions are actually signals from our internal guidance system (which I call the Inner Compass), which are giving us important information about ourselves. Because these signals from within are constantly telling us whether or not we are living in harmony with who we truly are – and whether or not we are living in respectful, healthy relationships with the other people in our lives (the Healthy Models for Relationships described in Part 1 of this book). So in brief, the better something feels, the more in alignment we are with our true selves and the more we are in alignment with the Healthy Models for Relationships. And the more discomfort we are feeling, the more out of alignment we are with our true selves and the more unhealthy or dysfunctional our relationships are.

This is the basic mechanism here and this is the true significance of our emotions. Our emotions are at all times giving us vital information as to whether or not we are living in alignment with who we truly are, with Healthy Models for Relationships and with the Nature of Reality.

So what happens when we don't listen to what our emotions are telling us and we ignore the signals we are getting from within? Firstly, these signals don't go away; rather they grow in intensity, get louder and become more powerful. This means when you ignore the significance of your emotions and especially when you ignore the feelings of discomfort you are experiencing, these signals try harder to get your attention. In other words, what started out as a vague feeling of mild discomfort will become a stronger feeling of discomfort. If you still don't heed the signals from within and understand the information these signals are giving you but continue to move away from harmonious living and what's best for you, these signals or emotions will get even stronger. So the unease and discomfort become more and more pronounced. More and more powerful. When this happens, people may start to feel really negative emotions such as nervousness, or anxiety, or fear, or depression, or irritation and anger. In other words, the feelings (emotions) get stronger.

This is where many people begin to look for ways to cope with their feelings of discomfort. Since most of us don't understand the real cause of our discomfort, or know what to do about it, we begin to develop various coping strategies to numb the pain of these uncomfortable emotions. It could be, for example, overeating or over-exercising or drinking or drugs or self-medicating – all in an attempt to ease the discomfort. Some people try to cope by losing themselves in work (and become workaholics), or in food (and develop eating disorders), or through shopping, gambling, sexing, or whatever. There are many ways we humans try to soothe ourselves when experiencing uncomfortable emotions. Many ways in which we try to soothe the uneasiness and anxiety we are feeling about ourselves and our lives, which arise from not listening to the signals from within and from being out of alignment with who we truly are and healthy living.

If we then continue to neglect the signals from within and continue to move away from being in alignment with who we really are – the next thing that happens is we start to get physical indicators of this lack of alignment. Symptoms such as headaches, backaches, stomachaches, muscular tension start to appear. All of these symptoms are indicators that we are not allowing and moving with the natural flow of energy in our lives. Indicators that show us that something is out of whack in our energy systems. At this stage of unease (dis-ease), the symptoms are usually not chronic and tend to move around – in other words, they come and go in relation to how much we move back and forth, or in and out of alignment.

Then finally, if we continue to disregard the signals from within, the signals will get even more powerful and may finally manifest as so-called "chronic" or "serious" illness. In this light, it is interesting to understand that so-called serious illness can still be understood to be a signal that we are out of alignment with who we really are, a signal that there is disharmony in our lives and relationships, as well as a sign that the energy is not flowing harmoniously in our system. As anyone who has studied the mind-body connection knows, our bodies tend to manifest and out-picture (reflect) what is going on inside us emotionally. So it makes perfect sense that when we disregard the signals coming from within, they will show up in various bodily symptoms that indicate a lack of alignment with the natural flow of energy and of Life.

Physical or emotional discomfort?

So let's try playing with this approach to physical discomfort and take a concrete example. Let's say you have indigestion or often have stomach discomfort after you eat, what is this telling you? How would or could we translate this physical sensation into what it feels like? Remember the above premise – that physical sensations are just an exaggerated form of emotion or emotions. So with this in mind, what does indigestion feel like? First of all we could say that the physical discomfort feels like, or is telling us, that there is something about what we are eating that we can't digest. Something which is not going down smoothly. This would probably be our most immediate answer. But if we go a little deeper (and instead of just thinking about the food we are eating and what we can't digest), we can ask ourselves more generally – what is there in my life right now (or before) that I can't digest? Is there something going on that I can't digest? Is there something or someone that doesn't agree with me? Something that isn't going down smoothly? And then see what comes up.

This is a fascinating way of regarding our physical sensations.

Or what about asking yourself – when did you first have this physical sensation? How far back can you trace it? Back five years or all the way back to your childhood? And then again the question is – what was going on in your life then that you couldn't digest? Ask yourself and see what comes up. It is often very enlightening to examine our physical sensations like this because we quickly discover that these sensations can provide us with very important clues and information as to what's going on in our lives (both past and present). In this way, we can discover that this energy, these physical sensations, these feelings are all messengers from within. They are all telling us something about what is going on with us. And they have always been there – both the feelings and the physical sensations. Which brings us to the real question... have we been listening? And if not, why not? Why haven't we been noticing and aware of this important information that is coming from within us? Because this information is always there and has always been there.

And then comes the next question: If the above is true, what can we do about it? First of all, we can try to address the issues that these emotions are signaling that are problematic in our lives. Such as a lack of healthy boundaries, difficulty saying no, perfectionism, unrealistic expectations to yourself and others – and so on. Which is basically what this whole book is about.

And secondly, because we have probably disregarded the

signals/emotions that these situations or problems triggered, we may have, in all likelihood, repressed these emotions and the energy behind them. And often for quite a long time. So as a result, this energy is stored within our bodies, and sooner or later, may manifest as unpleasant psychological and/or physical symptoms. Thus, the question arises – in addition to taking action apropos the problematic situations – what can we do to release the energy stored within our systems? This is where the technique I call emotional decompression can be very helpful.

Emotional decompression

Here is an exercise for getting in touch with what's going on within you. It will help you make contact with the energy that may be locked within your body. The exercise is called "emotional decompression", and it's easy to do and usually brings an immediate sense of relief – as well as new insights and information.

To do this exercise, you can either lie down flat on your back or sit comfortably in a chair. Lying down is preferable, if possible.

Now get as comfortable as you possibly can. And just take a deep breath and relax. Just let yourself sink into the mat or bed or ground or the chair you are sitting in. Just let go and relax. Once you feel comfortable, do what I call a "body scan". And by this I mean, just scan your body from head to toe slowly and just notice what you discover. Notice where in your body you feel a sense of ease and flow – and then notice if there are any areas where you feel tension or discomfort or any type of pain or blockages. You might feel tenseness or unease in several places – so just notice whatever discomfort or resistance is there. Just notice.

Now this exercise is not about making anything go away or about changing anything. It is only about noticing what is going on in your body and then just allowing and accepting whatever is happening there. There is no right or wrong way to do this, it's just about noticing and allowing and accepting.

Okay so let's say you have now scanned your body and you discover that you feel a sense of tightness or discomfort in your chest area. Okay, so that is what you discovered. So just allow it to be exactly as it is. Don't try to make it go away or change anything. Instead just notice what's going on and then try to explore this area a little bit more. So just look at and feel your chest area and the energy that is here.

Then ask yourself, how large is this area of discomfort? In other words, if you regard your chest area as an energy field, how big is this area? Does it go all the way up to your throat and down to your navel? Or is it more concentrated around your heart? How much space does it fill? And how far out to each side does this energy field go? Just notice how big the area is. Does it extend out in front of you or out in back of you? Again, just notice and allow and accept whatever you find. As I said before, there is no right or wrong way of doing this. It's just about noticing.

Now that you have ascertained the size of the energy field we are exploring, ask yourself what the temperature of this area is. Is it hot or cold? Or lukewarm? Or very cold? Just notice.

And what about colors? When you "look at" or "feel" this area, this energy field, do any colors come to mind? For example, is it flaming red or bright yellow or is the area dark or black or grey? What do you "see"? Whatever comes to mind is the right answer for you. So again, just allow and accept. Don't try to change anything or make it go away. Just let it be. Next notice the texture or consistency of this energy field you are exploring. Is it hard or soft? Firm or mushy? Muddy, watery, tight, sharp, jagged? Again, whatever comes to mind is the right answer for you. All we are doing here is zooming in on the energy and getting a "feeling" for what is going on in your body in this area.

So whatever comes up – just notice it and allow and accept it. Don't try to make anything go away... because you can't. No, you can't make any of these sensations go away. They just are what they are and they are where they are. All we are doing now is noticing them and allowing them to be exactly what they are. We are no longer resisting anything. Once you are "comfortable" with noticing this area of discomfort and have zoomed in on it a bit and are now allowing it to be whatever it is, try to go into it a little. Imagine you are an explorer or skilled detective like Sherlock Holmes, and that you are going to go into this energy field a little and see what's going on in there. So now try to just slowly ease yourself into the space in your chest and notice how it feels in there.

And once you are in there a little – ask yourself – how does it feel in here? What do you discover in here? Is there a feeling of sadness? Or fear? Or anger? Is there a feeling of frustration? What's the feeling in there? Do you discover a little child in there who is weeping or howling? Is there a scream in there? Is someone afraid in there? Or angry? Whatever you discover is fine. The key here is to allow and accept whatever comes up. Because we are just talking about energy. Energy that you have been suppressing, energy and emotions that you have not been aware of or in contact with – energy that wants to move and come out. So that is what we are doing and what we are going to do. Whatever comes up, whatever arises, you are now simply going to allow and accept this energy, allow this energy to arise and come out. You are going to release it.

If there is a cry or a howl or powerful feelings of sadness or anger – let it out. Let the energy out... let it go. And if you are (hopefully) somewhere where you can actually cry or express yourself – then do it. Let yourself groan, howl, weep, shout... whatever it is. It's just energy... energy that wants to come out. Energy that wants to circulate and move. Energy that perhaps has been suppressed for a long time and now wants to be released. That is why this exercise is called "emotional decompression" – because it's about noticing and then allowing whatever energy we have pent up inside of us to come out and be released. We are allowing the energy to be decompressed. And it's simply such a liberating and releasing thing to do. Because that is the nature of energy, it wants to move, always. And when energy is suppressed or repressed or held in, it always causes discomfort. So when we allow energy to move and flow again and be released, it always bring an immediate sense of relief. Always. It's as if we opened up a pressure cooker and let all the hot air escape... whoosh... it just feels so good... so wonderful, so liberating. People experience the most amazing healings when they do this exercise – they just do. When we get in touch with who we really are and how we really feel, we just feel so much better. This is truth telling at the highest level – because our bodies never lie. Never. They remember everything – even if we don't want to.

So just take a look at what's going on within you, and allow and accept whatever you find. And then see what happens.

Just do it.

Plus as you explore and poke around whatever area of your body or your energy field you are exploring, you will probably get some amazing insights into what's been going on with you. Old memories will come up, flashbacks will arise... pictures of situations or people will come to mind... so just remind yourself... whatever comes up – it's all okay. It's all you. And now all you have to do is allow and accept... whatever it is... just relax and let go... just let the energy come out, just let it decompress... and disappear... back into the nothingness from which it came.

Just do it.

And then just breathe... breathe deeply... aahhh...

Emotional decompression for specific issues

This brings us to another way of doing emotional decompression. Let's say you (or the person you are working with) are talking about or experiencing or dealing with an upsetting event or situation either now in your present life situation or in the past. We can also use emotional decompression to deal with the energy and discomfort that arises here. Let's say we're talking about a situation in which you have been shamed or blamed, and that you (or the person you are working with) either as a child or today as an adult did not know how to defend yourself and instead got a shock and felt (feel) bad. In situations like this, emotional decompression can be a highly effective tool for getting in touch with the energy that was blocked and in releasing it.

So start by thinking about being in the troubling situation (or asking the person who is doing the exercise to think about being in the troubling situation). Then ask... when you think about being in this situation and feel the discomfort of being in that situation, where exactly in the body do you feel the discomfort? Again, try to locate the discomfort. Do you feel it in your chest area? Or in your stomach area? Or in the throat? Or do you feel tension in your neck and shoulders when you think of what happened and feel the discomfort? Just notice.

Then when you have located the discomfort – when you can identify where it is located – do the exercise described on the preceding pages. So again, start by noticing how big the energy field is. How much space does it fill? Then notice the temperature – is it hot or cold or lukewarm? And does the energy field have a color or colors? And what about the texture of the energy field? Is it hard or soft, mushy or cloudy or like cement... and then go into the feeling of it. What does it feel like in there?

Go in there and just notice.

And again, just allow and accept whatever comes up.

If, as in our example above, you were unjustly shamed or

blamed for something that had nothing to do with you, how did it make you feel? Do you feel angry? Do you have a feeling of rage or anger all bottled up inside of you that is stuck in that place of discomfort you have now located in your physical body? If so, now is the time to let the energy out. Now is the time to release it. Now is the time to let the energy move. This energy is most probably your personal power that wants to come out, so now is the time to let it come out (for more about your personal power see Healthy Model no. 11). This energy is the natural, healthy impulse inside you to defend yourself in that situation – but because this energy was blocked, you still feel discomfort because the energy is still in there and it still wants to come out. So now is your chance – now is the time to let it come out. Now is the time. So just open the doors and let all the energy out. Just let it go. Just let it flow and run its course.

Notice – what does this energy really want to do? Does it want to shout at the person who shamed and blamed you and tell them they got it all wrong? That it had nothing to do with you? That they should grow up and take responsibility for their own lives instead of blaming things on you? If that's what's all pent up inside of you – then let it out. Say it out loud if you can. Just let the energy out. Emotionally, energetically, physically – and verbally if you can. Say what you want to say. Just do it.

As you let the energy out, if you feel (for example) like there's a volcano erupting from your stomach or chest, then let that volcano erupt, just let the energy out. Just allow and accept. Again, it's all about energy that is inside you that has been suppressed or blocked that wants to move and come out. So just let it come… just let it out. You will feel so much better when you do. This exercise always brings such an enormous sense of relief.

Some considerations when doing emotional decompression

Doing emotional decompression can be a very powerful experience, so it is wise to be in a safe space when you do it. And if you are doing this with someone, the person – whether a therapist or a friend – should be a safe person. Someone you trust, someone who supports you and someone who understands the exercise and what it's all about. It's also important to understand that it's all about energy. This is an energetic experience. And energy is not a dangerous thing although it can feel unpleasant at times. This is nothing to be afraid of, but it is important to understand that feelings and emotions, especially when they are very powerful, can be unpleasant for a while, but they're not dangerous, especially if you allow them to come out and decompress and be released. Also keep in mind that most people need to do this exercise more than once, in fact probably many times. This is because most of us have a great deal of old suppressed energy that is causing us discomfort and which we feel in various areas of our bodies without recognizing what it is. So doing emotional decompression one time, even though it helps a lot, is usually not enough. Most of us need to do it several or many times. The good news is that each time you do this exercise, you will release some more of the energy and feel immediate relief. But it's important to understand that you probably haven't released all of the energy you have suppressed over the years (in one or two goes). So there is probably more. And there might be much more. So just keep on doing it...

On the other hand, it's good to know there is only a finite amount of old energy stored within you, so each time you do release some of it, there is less of a backlog and so you just generally feel better and better. More at ease in your life. Plus you will begin to discover that even situations which might have upset you in the past just don't seem to upset you so much anymore. Why? Because you don't have such a backlog of old pent-up energy that gets triggered at the slightest irritation. And as a result, you will probably become much more easygoing in general, which is quite nice.

The pressure cooker effect and emotional decompression

It can help to imagine or envision our stored or repressed emotions as energy that is stored up in a pressure cooker. You know what a pressure cooker is, don't you? It is a way of cooking food in a pot which has a very, very snug lid which is screwed on very tightly to keep all the steam inside the pot. When we use a pressure cooker, we keep all the energy locked inside the pot. Well, when we repress or suppress our emotions, it works the same way. We are keeping our emotions/energy inside of us under a tight lid. We're not letting the energy (these emotions) out and we're not letting them flow freely. In other words, we are blocking the energy. Often with uncomfortable emotional and so-called "physical" consequences (as described in the beginning of this chapter). Why do we do this? We do this because of all the reasons already mentioned in this book. In addition, we do this because we have been programmed to believe we should be calm under all circumstances. We do this because we believe in a lot of "shoulds" about the way we should think and feel which don't harmonize with reality. We do this because of all the flawed premises we believe in. All of which causes a great deal of discomfort or negative emotion. But because we don't believe or understand why we feel the way we do, we repress or suppress our true feelings because they are not "acceptable" or so we have been taught to believe. Unfortunately, when we do this – when we suppress or repress our emotions – it's like putting a tight lid on a pressure cooker. We are keeping our emotions and the energetic charge locked tightly inside of us. And the more we do this, the more we keep the lid tightly on, the more pressure there builds up and the more discomfort – and often physical discomfort – we experience.

Then, on top of all this, because we have so much repressed emotion, we may become afraid of our own discomfort and our own feelings. And then, this fear of our own discomfort may trigger the "fight or flight" response in our bodies which just tends to increase our discomfort. See the next Healing Process No. 5 about *Dealing With Anxiety* to get a better understanding of what happens when you inadvertently trigger the "fight or flight" response in your body and become afraid of your own feelings. So to avoid getting trapped in this misunderstanding, the key here is to understand that what you are experiencing is not dangerous, that it's all energy, and that the best way to deal with what you are experiencing is to just "allow and accept" whatever you are feeling.

But in general, it is important to keep reminding ourselves that the basic principle here is that the more we close down and repress our emotions, the more momentum this repressed energy gains and the more discomfort we may feel which, as I said before, usually manifests as physical discomfort or physical symptoms since we often won't allow ourselves to feel our emotions.

The short version

The short version of all this is, the more you repress how you feel, the more energy or momentum these feelings gain and the more you may begin to feel uncomfortable about what's going on with you.

When we do emotional decompression, we are actually doing the opposite. Instead of closing down, we are actually opening the doors to our emotions a bit by slightly opening the valve on top of the pressure cooker – and letting some of the steam out. And then what happens? Well, as everyone knows, when you first open the valve on top of a pressure cooker, there's a big whoosh and all this steam comes out in a powerful stream. But in a few seconds, it's basically over. The steam has been released and there is no more pressure. And that's what happens when we do emotional decompression. We "let off steam" so to speak in a safe, controlled environment. And as soon as the steam has dissipated, we feel relief.

The other point to remember is no one gets rid of all the steam they have stored up inside of themselves in one go. It takes time and a bit of repeating this exercise. But each time you do emotional decompression, the amount of steam or repressed energy you have left or still stored inside of you is less. So slowly, slowly you feel better and better until one day... there's less pressure inside and it's almost all gone! Oh happy day!

There are also many other good ways to release the old energy we may have stored in our systems. For example, if you are feeling a lot of anger, you can go out in the woods and try throwing branches at a dead tree trunk to get the energy out. Or you can even envision that the tree trunk is the person or people who have treated you so badly. Or if you are at home, you can imagine the person sitting on a chair or in your bed and then throw pillows at them. Or you can even try letting the energy out by punching a boxing bag. For some, going for a brisk run or even vigorously cleaning the house or apartment can help let some of the old, pent-up energy out.

And one final word: Please understand and remember that underneath all of this old energy we may have stored in our systems, is our innate, inherent worth and Original Goodness. Yes, indeed, inside each one of us is a Wonder Child, our True Selves, that each one of us was from the very beginning. And when we begin to see, understand and experience this... then it's oh happy day indeed.

Healing Process No. 5

Dealing With Anxiety

Being nervous and at times anxious is part of being human. Most people experience varying degrees of nervousness or anxiousness during the course of their lives. It's part of the human condition for most of us. Recognizing this is a good way of taking care of ourselves and living sanely.

Sometimes this nervousness may become more intense and then we call the feelings we are experiencing – anxiety. Many people experience varying degrees of anxiety – and again this is a very normal, human experience. Unfortunately, anxiety is still a big taboo in our society (for most people), and as a result, many people suffer in silence from this perfectly human predicament. If this is the case with you – if you sometimes experience anxiety that gets very intense – you may not be getting the help you deserve because you are ashamed of feeling anxious or having panic attacks. This is unfortunate because understanding what anxiety is and what triggers it can be a great help in demystifying and dealing sanely and appropriately with it. So that's what I'd like to do here – I'd like to try to demystify anxiety and offer some sane ways to deal with it.

Let's start by looking at what anxiety is.

The human body is designed – like all animals – to react quickly to danger. When faced with a physical threat or danger, we (like animals) automatically go into the "fight or flight" response. Which means if a tiger is after you or you're about to get hit by a bus, your body will react instantly and automatically to the perceived threat or danger by secreting adrenaline and cortisone which immediately alter the bodily functions to prepare you to either "fight"/defend yourself or "flight"/run away to escape the danger. Immediately the heart beats faster and the muscles contract and many ordinary functions (like digestion) get put on standby because they are not necessary in the present danger situation.

This is a perfectly normal physical reaction to danger and it's something we all experience automatically when threatened. It's important to understand that this is a physical mechanism that is part of the way our bodies function. It happens to everyone when faced with danger and it's perfectly normal. It's not something we can control or stop – it happens automatically. It's the way we are built. Our bodies react automatically to thoughts of "danger".

It's also important to understand that this inbuilt "fight or flight" response is actually our friend, the evolutionary response of all humans and animals which is designed to ensure our survival. Without this automatic, inbuilt "fight or flight" response, we humans and most animals would not be here today. In other words, this response has ensured our survival in the face of danger throughout all of animal and human evolution.

There is, however, one big difference between us humans and animals – and that is – we humans are "thinking" creatures. This means that we (unlike animals) can imagine (think of) the future. Which also means we can imagine, visualize, and conceive of possible danger or a threat in the future that has not yet arisen. And this is very important to understand. We can imagine things that haven't happened yet – and we can also imagine things that never will happen (something we often do, especially if we worry a lot and suffer from anxiety). And this is where the problem of anxiety arises. When we are anxious and suffer from anxiety and/or panic attacks – we believe in an imminent threat (whether or not this is the reality). And as a result of this thought/belief in an imminent threat – we unwittingly trigger the "fight or flight" response in our own bodies. When this happens, our bodies automatically go into high alert (because this is how our bodies are designed to react to danger) whether we are at a party, sitting in a business meeting, or just buying milk at the supermarket. Then, as a result of this high alert mechanism being triggered, we also experience all the bodily changes that are triggered by the "fight or flight" response.

But here's the problem. Since there is no clear and present danger – since there is no tiger about to attack you in the supermarket – you have what we call an anxiety attack or a panic attack, which is really just experiencing all the physical symptoms of the "fight or flight" mechanism without having a real physical threat to deal with. In other words, without having to "fight"/defend yourself or "flight"/run away. But it happens anyway because your brain had a fear thought which triggered this response in your body. Once you had the thought, it happened automatically.

So then what happens?

Because adrenaline and cortisone are released into the system it is highly likely that you may experience some or many of the following physical symptoms: your heart beats more rapidly, your pulse increases, you go weak in the knees, your hands shake, your perceptions change, you may feel a sense of unreality, you may feel dizzy/shaky, you may feel butterflies in your stomach, or you might even feel nauseous... In other words, you experience a host of physical symptoms, all triggered by the "fight or flight" mechanism. But since there's no tiger after you because you are just sitting there at the meeting or standing in line in the supermarket, you cannot use this energy as it was meant to be used. In other words, you cannot use this energy by fighting or running away, so instead you end up wondering what all these strange physical symptoms are about. Because all you're doing is buying milk in the supermarket – or listening to your boss delegating work assignments.

Then comes the next unsettling bit: You may get alarmed or scared of what you are feeling. You may get alarmed or be scared by what's happening to you and the physical sensations you are experiencing. Scared of your body and its reaction, and you might wonder – what's wrong with me? Why am I feeling so strange? Why am I sweating like this? Why is my heart racing? Why do I feel dizzy? Am I having a heart attack? Is there something wrong with me? What's going on?

So now you are afraid of your own initial response to whatever the perceived danger or threat was (which in this case was only a thought in your mind). But now that you have triggered the "fight or flight" response in your body and you are not using the energy that is released to defend yourself or run away, you just experience all these sensations in your body, and if that also frightens you, then you may have a full-blown panic attack. Now let's just stop a minute and examine this sequence of events very slowly because this is extremely important when it comes to learning to deal with anxiety and panic attacks.

The full-blown anxiety or panic attack (like the scenario I just described) actually has two distinct parts. Although it all happens so quickly most people don't realize this. There is the first part of the panic attack – and then there's the second part. The first part is when something (either a thought about an event or a thought) triggers the initial fear and the "fight or flight" response. This trigger could be a certain situation (like real danger or just going to a meeting or a party or having to stand up and speak in front of a group of people) – there are many possibilities. (It could even be the thought that you might have a panic attack in a certain situation.) And then there's the second part of the anxiety/panic attack – which is when you become afraid of your own initial response and what your body is doing. When you become afraid of your rapidly beating heart, churning stomach, feelings of shakiness, etc.

We can call these two parts of your response – *first fear* and *second fear*. So first fear is the initial trigger and second fear is when you are afraid of your own response. In other words, the second part is – *fear of fear.*

Second fear = *fear of fear*

Now this is very important to understand: When you become afraid of your initial response and what your body is doing – in other words, when you feel a fear of fear rush and the following physical activation (rapid heartbeat, sweating, feeling shaky) – you are actually experiencing what we call *second fear.* And here comes the important part: This second fear is actually prolonging the "fight or flight" reaction in your body because by being afraid of your initial response (rapid heartbeat, etc.), you trigger your body to continue secreting adrenaline. And as a result, the high alert condition continues. The "fight or flight" activation continues.

People who suffer from anxiety and feel desperate about their condition have usually been triggering this mechanism in their bodies so consistently over such a long period of time that they are now in what I call "a constant state of high arousal". And unfortunately, once you're in a constant state of high arousal, it takes very little to trigger the "fight or flight" response in your body because your system is now so over-sensitized. In fact, just the slightest thing can set off a new rush of adrenaline into the system – the slightest thought. For example, just the thought of some future event or just the thought of meeting people or of going to the supermarket... and then you're caught in the grip of anxiety because since you don't understand what's going on with you, you continue to keep triggering this mechanism in your own body. It's fear upon fear upon fear, and all because you are afraid of the "fight or flight" mechanism, which is a perfectly natural, normal, automatic physical response that all creatures have.

But here's the good news – when you understand this – you can find your way out of this intensely challenging and difficult conundrum! For some people, just understanding what is going on is enough to cure them!

What you can do

So what can we do about all this? I suggest a two-pronged approach to the challenge comprising what I call "first aid" and "reality testing".

First aid

The first approach is what I call "first aid" because it can be used to deal with the immediate anxiety and/or panic attacks. This technique helps you manage the second fear or the fear of fear itself.

Reality testing

The second approach is what I call "reality testing" because this involves the long-term process of identifying and questioning the "catastrophic thinking" that is triggering the original "fight or flight" mechanism to begin with. This approach deals with first fear – or the original mindset and underlying beliefs that trigger fear in you in the first place.

(Before we look at these two approaches, let me make it clear that if you are in any way worried about your physical health – for example your heart – it is very important that you go to the doctor and get a thorough physical checkup first. The physical symptoms triggered by the "fight or flight" mechanism can mimic the physical symptoms of other physical ailments, so before you begin using the techniques described here, it's important that you get checked by your doctor first and are told you are in good health and that "there's nothing physically wrong with you".)

First aid

When you're feeling anxiety or having a panic attack, I suggest using Dr. Claire Weekes' formula for dealing with nervous illness. Her formula has 4 steps:

Facing
Accepting
Floating
Letting time pass

Let's look at her four steps.

Facing

Facing means understanding what is happening. Read and reread the above description of the "fight or flight" mechanism until you truly understand what it is and understand that it is a perfectly normal biological reaction to perceived danger. Next, remind yourself that by resisting or trying to suppress your symptoms (the fight or flight mechanism) you are only making things worse. Because by being afraid of the physical sensations, you prolong them because when you are afraid, you add more adrenaline to your system which then triggers the whole fight or flight syndrome again and again. So facing means standing there, understanding what's going on, and not resisting what is happening. Facing means understanding that you have been bluffed by physical symptoms of no medical significance. Facing means understanding that what you are experiencing is unpleasant – but not dangerous. Facing means understanding that basically all your symptoms mean nothing! It is just the activation of the fight or flight mechanism in your body.

Accepting

Accepting means acceptance – and this is the key to dealing with anxiety and panic attacks when they arise – and getting over them. Accepting means just letting it happen. Not resisting. It means understanding and knowing what is going on. It means understanding and knowing that what your body is doing is perfectly normal and natural, and then allowing your body to do what it does. When you accept what is going on, *you do not add second fear to the original first fear.* And when you do not add second fear to the symptoms you are experiencing, you are not triggering the secretion of more adrenaline and cortisone into your system, so the physical activation of the "fight or flight" mechanism will lessen and then finally stop. When you accept, you just watch your heart race and your knees knock and you're not afraid of this happening. You know it's not dangerous. You know it's a perfectly normal physical mechanism that has been triggered in you because of some fear thought.

So you just accept what's going on. And you realize that resisting (which is second fear) will only make it worse, will only make your symptoms continue (because it triggers the secretion of more adrenaline and cortisone into your system). And because you know this will only make you even more sensitive and hyper-aroused. This is the heart of the cure. Acceptance. True acceptance. Just letting it all happen.

Floating

Floating is the physical out-picturing or manifestation of acceptance. Floating means allowing your body to relax with your mind, it means letting go of all tension in your body because when you start to become aware of what you're doing when you have a panic attack, you will see that you are tensing up. You are tensing up because you are fighting the sensations you are having. Floating is the opposite of fighting and resisting. Floating is just letting go. Floating means to have no physical resistance. It's like you are lying on your back in a lovely swimming pool and just floating in the warm sunshine.

You're completely relaxed physically, doing nothing. So this is a way of allowing your body to calm down. Just let all your muscles relax and go limp. First you accept what is happening in your mind, and then you allow your body to float and release all tension.

Letting time pass

The last step is letting time pass. This is so important because recovering from anxiety and the nervous tension it generates in the body takes time. This means that even if you now understand what is happening to you right now, and accept and float and don't resist anything, you will probably still go on feeling anxious and panicky for a while – simply because your system is so worked up. When you have been in a state of high arousal for a long time (which most people who are suffering from anxiety and panic attacks are), it takes a while for the nervous system to calm down again. Because you are over-sensitized and this doesn't just disappear in one day. This means you will have to keep practicing *facing*, *accepting* and *floating* for a while before your general, overall arousal level starts to go down. That is why it is so important not to be impatient. If you're impatient and want immediate results, it really means you are still resisting and not accepting all your symptoms as normal and natural. Because if you did, if you accepted that all your symptoms were normal and nature, why would you be in such a hurry, why would you be so impatient?

So again, when panic strikes – practice these 4 steps.

Facing
Accepting
Floating
Letting time pass

They work wonders if given a fair chance. For more about Dr. Claire Weekes' technique, see any of her many books such as *Essential Help for Your Nerves* or *Peace from Nervous Suffering*. I am sure you will find all her books very helpful and comforting.

Right Reaction Readiness

To make it even more clear how to deal with stress, anxiety and panic attacks, here is a simple exercise you can do anywhere at any time:

Right Reaction – the Exercise:

The moment you experience stress symptoms and/or have a panic attack and/or experience anxiety symptoms such as:

- A fear flash
- An electric jolt through your body
- A heat flash (feeling suddenly very hot)
- Heart beating rapidly (heart palpitations)
- Heart pounding forcefully
- That trembly-shaky feeling
- Feeling that the body goes weak
- Weak, shaky legs
- Chest pains
- Muscular tension
- Tension in neck and shoulders
- Feel unsteady or unbalanced
- Nausea
- Stomach discomfort (churning stomach)
- Feel muzzy headed (feel foggy in your head)
- Feel a sense of unreality

Here's what to do:

1) Stop immediately and take a deep breath
2) Breathe out slowly
3) Let your whole body slacken, slump and sag
4) Let everything become loose (let all your muscles relax)
5) Focus on where you are
6) Take another deep breath
7) Breathe out slowly
8) And then slowly go on with whatever you are doing regardless of how you are feeling instead of recoiling in fear and resisting how you feel
9) Float forward with whatever you are doing
10) It's okay to move forward slowly, but move forward
11) Slacken those reins, don't try to stop yourself from feeling what you are feeling
12) Move forward slowly with as little muscular tension and resistance as possible
13) No need to rush
14) If necessary, take some more deep breaths

Repeat this exercise as often as you need to during the course of your day. Relaxing and letting go are an actual physiological process which eventually calms the body because when you don't resist the fear flashes, the body stops secreting more adrenaline into the system and eventually calms down. But it is important to understand that this calming effect rarely happens immediately because the body is so sensitized (hypervigilant), so you have to keep practicing Right Reaction Readiness for a while before you can expect to really feel the results.

Reality testing

Using the above exercise and the Claire Weekes technique above to deal with anxiety and panic attacks when they occur is very effective, and for many, it may be enough to lessen and even cure their anxiety attacks.

But if it isn't, it makes sense to embark on what I call *Reality testing*. And by this I mean embarking on the process of identifying and investigating the underlying thoughts and beliefs that are making you afraid to begin with. Why can this be so important? Because it is your thinking that is the cause of your fears and not the events themselves. (See Basic Observations 1 and 2 for more about this mechanism.) In other words, thinking is the cause, and fear and anxiety are the effects of your beliefs and interpretation of situations.

If you are in doubt about this, let's take a simple example.

Let's say going to a meeting triggers great anxiety or even panic in you. Obviously this has nothing to do with the reality of going to the meeting itself because the 10 other people who are sitting around the table aren't having panic attacks (at least not as far as you know). So it is not the meeting itself that is causing your panic but your thoughts about the meeting situation. In other words, you must have some thoughts or some interpretation of this situation that makes you find it "dangerous" for you in some way – thoughts that trigger the "fight or flight" mechanism in you. It could be because you don't like speaking in front of a group. It could be because you're insecure about your appearance or your weight. It could be because you're worried about what other people will think of you. It could be… a million and one things that trigger your anxiety – but it's not inherent in the situation itself. It's in your thinking about the situation. So this is what *reality testing* is about. It's about looking at the difference between reality and your thinking. Again read and reread the Basic Observations in Part 2 of this book and keep contemplating the

Healthy Models described in Part 1 (such as Healthy Model No. 15: *Life Is a Learning Curve and We Are All Evolving*) – so you slowly become a little more realistic about what it means to be a human being.

In brief, reality testing is about finding out and identifying what thoughts or beliefs trigger anxiety in you. What thoughts arise in your mind right before you feel anxious? What is it about life and your present situation that triggers fear in you? Why are you so insecure in this situation? What is it, for example, about going to meetings that scares you? Or what is it about attending events or going to parties that make you feel so insecure or afraid? What is it about you and about these situations that trigger anxiety in you? Probably when you start to investigate what is going on you will discover that the situations you fear are the ones that trigger your deepest insecurities. In this connection, we are usually talking about the uninvestigated beliefs you have been carrying around since childhood.

Uncovering and investigating our belief systems is a process – and reading and meditating upon the Basic Observations in Part 2 of this book as well as the Healthy Models in Part 1 can be a tremendous help. This is because unless we are able to identify and investigate the flawed premises we believe in, we will probably continue to experience some degree of anxiety over and over again because we will continue to think and believe in the same thoughts over and over again. That is why going deeper and doing serious *reality testing* is such an excellent way to achieve real and lasting recovery from anxiety and panic attacks.

If you have difficulty doing this type of *reality testing* on your own, you may need professional help to uncover and identify the basic beliefs and flawed premises that are bothering you. If this is the case, going to a trained therapist, coach or counselor can be a great help. But whether you are working on your own or with a therapist, the basic exercise is the same – to compare reality with your thinking. And to uncover the flawed premises that are stressing you. Perhaps you are thinking thoughts like you "should" be so perfect (see Healthy Model No. 16 about *Moderation*) or you feel you should have all the answers (see Healthy Model No. 15 about *Life Is a Learning Curve*). Or perhaps the belief that is freaking you out is it will be terrible if you make a mistake (again see Healthy Model No. 15).

Continue to keep checking on what is going on with you and ask yourself regularly: Is the reality you are facing half as bad, dangerous, unmanageable, or uncertain as you believe it to be? Stop and look at the facts. Look at the reality. And once you've done that – notice that if you are realistic, you will probably discover that you actually do have the resources required to more or less manage the situation. (For more about how to focus on your strengths and resources, see Healing Process No. 7: *Using the Power of Mind Wisely for Healing and Recovery*.)

This means that if you keep working with the thoughts and beliefs that are stressing you, you will gradually realize that:

- It's not really the end of the world.
- So much of what you are saying and thinking has nothing to do with reality.
- So much of what you are thinking is mental over-exaggeration or "catastrophic" thinking.
- It's you, you yourself, who is continually triggering the "fight or flight" mechanism in your own body.

The good news here is that once you can see, identify and understand this mechanism and how you are triggering the "fight or flight" mechanism in your own body, you can actually do something about it. So take the time to think deeply about these things and watch what you are doing. And when you can actually see what's going on, then you can slowly take your power back and gradually stabilize yourself and your nervous system using a combination of the two approaches outlined above – *First aid* and *Reality testing*.

Healing Process No. 6

The Difference Between Reality and Your Expectations

As outlined in the first Basic Observations in Part 2 of this book – there is "reality" and then there is our thinking about reality. These are two different things. Reality is what it is. Reality is the way things are. Reality is the way people are. People are who they are. And then there's our thinking about this reality as well as our expectations to this reality. And they are often quite different or very different.

And this is where problems can arise for us because: *The greater the gap or difference between reality and our expectations to reality, the more we suffer.* That's the mechanism. Because when we expect reality to be different than what it is, we are resisting reality and we always lose. Because reality is what it is. That means reality always wins. However, this does not mean we cannot ask for what we want. We all have our preferences and wishes, and a part of healthy self-care is being able to ask for what we want or prefer in a respectful manner. But once we have asked for what we want or prefer, it's up to the other person, or other people, to respond. In other words, by their words and their actions (or lack of words and actions), other people will be saying yes or no to our wishes and preferences. Once we have this information, then we can decide what course of action is the wisest for us – based on the reality of who another person is (or how other people are) – instead of being lost in the dream of how we think things or people "should" be.

Reality is what it is

So… reality is what it is – that's the deal. People and things are what they are. That's the way of it.

Now when we take a specific situation or a specific relationship, again we have the reality of it. The reality of what is going on or how this person or people are behaving. In other words, what they are actually saying and doing. That's the reality. And then we each have our own expectations, thoughts and ideas about the situation or person or people involved.

Then if our expectations or preferences are very different from reality, it can be very painful or disappointing or stressful for us. In other words, the greater the difference between reality (the way things are) and our expectations to the way things are or our beliefs about how reality should be, the more unhappy, dissatisfied, upset, frustrated, angry, anxious, or depressed we feel. In other words, the bigger the gap between reality and our expectations, the more we suffer.

Unfortunately, most of us have many unrealistic expectations to life, to other people, to ourselves, to our bodies, to our feelings, and to our interactions with other people. And all of these unrealistic expectations can make life highly stressful.

Now why is this so? Because getting back to the way things are – reality is what it is. People are the way they are. We don't have a say in this. We don't have a choice. Again, if you look closely at what is going on, people don't just up and change because you or I think they "should". It doesn't work like that. People are the way they are. Even if we ask them to change or to do things differently, they often can't or won't or aren't interested. And regardless of how unfortunate this might seem to you or me, this is just the way it works. This is the setup here in this life experience, which is why it's a good idea to take a good look at the reality of situations and the people involved, and notice what's really going on. Notice what the situation really is or how this person really is – because then you can adjust your expectations and be much more realistic about what's going on. This also means you will have a much better chance of dealing with things realistically and wisely. And as

The Difference Between Reality and Your Expectations

a result, you will suffer less! Because as long as you are lost in some dream or illusion about how you think things "should" be, you are not really present and almost always will have a hard time dealing with what is going on calmly and wisely. Because you are shadowboxing with illusions, lost in a dream world that doesn't exist. When this happens, you always lose – because again, reality rules.

The opposite is also true. Things quite simply go better when the gap or difference between reality (what's going on) and our expectations is less. In other words, when the gap between reality and our expectations is smaller, life becomes more manageable. And again, this doesn't mean that we can't have our preferences and wishes and ask for what we want. But once we've asked – and the other person or people have responded, either by their words or actions – or lack of actions – then that is the reality we have to deal with.

Women and relationships

Let's get a little more specific and look at an area where unrealistic expectations are sabotaging so many people and their lives – and that's women and relationships!

I coach a lot of people every day, and many people, especially women, have unrealistic expectations to the men in their lives, expectations which are often very far from reality. This is why I frequently say to the women who come to me – it's a really good idea to notice who their partner really and truly is. And not get lost in the dream of some man they'd like him to be, or who they're dreaming he'll become, but rather take a look at the man who is actually standing there, right before them. The man he actually is. "But oh," women often say, "he has so much potential." Or they'll say, "Things would be great if only he would..." or, "I know he said that, but he really means..."

And I always say, "Whoa, girl! Let's just slow down for a moment and examine what you are doing because this is never going to work." Why? Because it has nothing to do with reality. No, you are somewhere off in dreamland – and that never works because it's all mind stuff, fluff – just some thoughts in your head which end up making you miserable because they have nothing to do with what's happening right before your eyes. So stop it and drop it! Much, much better, much, much wiser to look at the man who is actually here, the man who is standing right before you – and then listen to what he's saying and watch what he's doing! And don't assume that you know better than he does what he's thinking or feeling. Because you don't! How could you? You are not inside his head, so you can't know what's really going on in there. (If you are in doubt about this, see the Basic Observations in Part 2 of this book.)

So look at him and listen to what he says, and then watch what he does – and relate to that. Notice what's going on and how it makes you feel. And if you're in doubt about what he's saying or doing, then ask him what he means and what's going on – but stop assuming that you know better than he does what he's thinking and feeling. In other words, relate to the real person, the actual man, who is standing right there before you – not some dream of a man who doesn't exist. Once you do this, it will be a whole lot easier for you to navigate realistically and wisely in life and make wise choices for yourself. Because the reality is – most people don't change. Be especially mindful of Observation 8 *You Can't "Fix" or Control or Change Another Person*. And when you understand this, it will be much easier for you to be more realistic – and then you will know what to do.

Expectations versus Reality – the exercise

To help you get better at identifying and closing the gap between reality and your expectations, I have developed the following exercise which I call "Expectations versus Reality". I've done this exercise with large groups and also in one-to-one sessions with clients. So I know from experience that it's always an eye-opener for people and very effective.

The exercise has four steps. You can do this exercise on your own or with another person. Since this exercise is about "Expectations versus Reality" in your couple relationship, I suggest you do not do this with your partner because it is important to be able to be completely honest. It's okay if you do it with a friend, as long as it's someone you can really be honest with.

If you are not in a relationship at the moment, you can still do this exercise and learn a lot. Do it on your ex-partner. And if you've never had a relationship, do it on your mother. Mothers work just as well.

Now please get out a piece of paper.

Step one: Expectations and wishes

Close your eyes and think of at least three things you think (or wish) your present partner would or should do (or that your ex-partner should have done). Think of three important things you think he or she should do now or should have done in the past that would make (or have made) your relationship better.

Here are some examples of what I mean. You might feel:

- He should spend more time with the children. (Or he should have.)
- He should stop drinking (he shouldn't drink so much).
- He should understand me better.
- He should be interested in the things I'm interested in.

Once you have thought of three important things that you really believe he or she should do that would make your relationship better, write the three things down on a piece of paper. (If you are doing this alone, you can, of course, write down more than three things.) If you are doing this exercise with another person, then take turns telling each other about the three things you wrote on your list. When you are listening to the other person tell about his or her three things, don't offer your opinion as to whether he/she is right or wrong. Just listen and allow the other person to tell you his or her story.

Step two: Reality

The next step in the exercise is to close your eyes and think of what the reality is compared to the three things you wrote on your list. Really go there. Look at what the actual situation is in relation to your expectations or wishes. Once you have identified what the reality is about each of your expectations, write this down on your paper.

In terms of the examples I gave above in Step one, the reality could look like this:

- He doesn't spend a lot of time with the children. (Or he does play with the children sometimes, but not as much as I would like.)
- He drinks a lot. (Or he drinks too much. Or he has a serious alcohol problem.)
- He doesn't understand me. (Or sometimes he understands me. He doesn't understand the things that are really important to me.)
- He's not interested in the things I'm interested in. (Or sometimes he is interested and sometimes not. It depends on what it is.)

If you are doing this exercise with another person, take turns telling each other about the reality compared to your expectations. Tell in detail what you discovered when you looked at the way things really are. And again, when you are listening to the other person tell about his or her reality, just listen and allow the other person to tell you what he or she discovered. There is no right and wrong here. This is just an exploration of the way things are.

Step three: Feelings

In step three, close your eyes and imagine how you would feel about your relationship and your partner if you were realistic. How would you feel if you accepted what the reality is? How would you feel if you didn't have any expectations or wishes that anything should be different from what it is? How would this feel? Go into the feelings. I have discovered that this step of the exercise can take a little time. It can take a little time to locate how you would feel if you related to the way things really are. This is because so many of our feelings about our relationships are actually linked to our expectations. We feel upset or sad or angry because of our expectations, so in this step, when you take away your expectations, what do you actually feel? Try to find that…

Then once you've found how that makes you feel, please write down these feelings. It can often be an eye-opener to discover one would feel quite differently!

If you are working with another person, now tell each other about the feelings you discovered when you thought about how you would feel if you accepted reality when it comes to the way your partner really is. And once again, no judgments, just listen to each other.

Step four: Action

The last step of the exercise is to look at what these discoveries lead to. So close your eyes again. Now that you've really felt what it would feel like if you accepted things the way they really are, how are you going to act? What actions do these feelings make you want to take? If you stick to reality, what will you do? What will you do differently right now if you look reality in the eye and forget your expectations and wishes? And especially when you keep in mind the Basic Observations in this book – and the understanding that we can't control other people and make them change.

If you are doing this exercise on an ex-partner, when you go back into the past, try to find how you would have acted differently in your former relationship if you really had looked at reality and acted accordingly. What would you have done differently?

Now write down what you discover. What will you do – and especially what you will do differently than what you're doing now (or what you did in the past)? This is called waking up to reality! This is "getting real". This is looking at what is and dealing with it – instead of living in some dream world. Sit with your discoveries for a while. How does this feel?

If you are doing the exercise with another person, talk to this person about the actions that come to mind that you feel are realistic in terms of reality. What is the realistic thing for you to do now?

I have noticed that people make wildly different discoveries when doing this exercise. Some people discover a new sense of appreciation for their partners – a new kindness – when they look at who their partners really are (instead of their stories about their partners). Some people say they are going to be much more appreciative and loving in the future. Others say that now they're definitely going to leave their partner because it's so obvious that things are never going to change! While others get new insights into ways that they can perhaps improve their way of communicating with their partners.

Whatever you do find, welcome to reality. It was there all along. It was just us who didn't notice.

Healing Process No. 7

Using the Power of Mind Wisely for Healing and Recovery

Over the last three decades, I have written many books about the incredible power of mind. In each book I have shared many practical tools and exercises for using the power of our minds wisely to live happier, more satisfying lives. These books include *The Road to Power – Fast Food for the Soul*, *The Mental Laws* and *The Awakening Human Being – A Guide to the Power of Mind* – just to name a few. Now, in this chapter, I'd like to share some of the ways we can use the power of our minds for self-empowerment and support during the healing and recovery processes we are talking about in this section of the book.

There are many, many ways we can do this, and I will try to outline a few powerful techniques for you in this section. But before we look at these techniques let us first briefly review the way our minds work and what this means for us in practice...

The incredible power of mind

Once we begin to understand that all our experiences are subjective, mental experiences, we can also start to recognize and appreciate the incredible power of our minds. So with this understanding, let us examine how we can use this amazing power of our minds more wisely – because this is the big issue.

It is not really a question of whether or not our thoughts and belief systems are determining our experiences of reality, because they are. But rather a question of understanding how we are doing this, and what we can do to improve the experiences we are living as a result of our thoughts and belief systems. Because like it or not, our thoughts and beliefs are the determining factor in our everyday experience of life. This means if we want to improve our life situations, we have to examine the ways in which we are using the power of our mind.

For most of us, up until now, the way our thoughts determine our experiences has been an unconscious process. But now many of us are waking up and are beginning to see and understand how this process works. Many are beginning to see that this is an impersonal mechanism and understand that our thoughts do, in fact, determine our experiences. And this discovery – the power of our thoughts – is one of the most important discoveries any human being can ever make. Because with this understanding, we begin to realize that we actually do always have a choice about the ways in which we relate to the world around us. And this is because we are the only thinkers in our minds, which means we can examine our thinking and choose to change the focus of our attention if what we discover does not serve us well. Because the basic law of mind says – *whatever you focus your attention on grows in your experience.*

This Universal Law is so important, I will repeat it again to make sure you notice this and think about what this means. So here it is again: **WHATEVER YOU FOCUS YOUR ATTENTION ON GROWS IN YOUR EXPERIENCE.**

The next very important point here is that when it comes to the focus of our attention – *we all do have a choice.* And again, this is an observation of major importance so I will repeat it again. You have a choice when it comes to the focus of your attention because you are the only thinker in your mind! And this is good news indeed! Because it means that once you wake up and understand the mechanism of mind, you no longer need to be the innocent, unconscious victim of your own thinking. On the contrary. You can, if you so desire, change the focus of your attention (and thus change your experiences) because you are the only thinker in your mind.

Becoming the conscious Choice-Maker in your life

Now you have the key to freedom because when you understand that you can consciously choose to change the focus of your attention, you can also change your life experience – moment by moment by moment. Which means that in every now moment, we can choose how we are going to use the incredible mind power that has been given us. We have a choice as to whether or not we are just going to habitually fall into our old programming and keep repeating the same old negative, stressful thought patterns and continue living the same life experiences. Or we can choose to be mindful and observe what's going in our minds, and then use the full power that is given us to step back and question the validity of our thoughts. And then change the thought stream if we find that the thoughts we are entertaining do not serve us. This is the choice that is facing us each and every day. This is what self-empowerment is all about. It's about asking yourself these questions every day:

- Am I going to step back and look at the thoughts I am holding in mind?
- Am I going to be conscious of what I am focusing my attention on, right now, today?
- Am I going to ask myself if the thoughts I am focusing on are in any way true?
- Am I going to ask myself if these thoughts and belief systems are serving me well?
- Are they creating the life experiences that I want to live?
- And if not – what am I going to do about it?
- Do I have the courage to take my power back and take control of my thinking?
- Do I have the courage to recognize that I am responsible for my own experience of life? Especially now that I know that whatever I am focusing on, whatever I am thinking

and believing with conviction, I am also experiencing in my life… as my life.

This is the choice before each one of us, each and every day. Because the truth is: *the focus of your attention determines your experience.* Yesterday, today and tomorrow. This is why to see and understand the way the mind works – is the key to freedom and liberation – for everyone! This is the key to self-empowerment. And nothing is more exciting than this discovery because it means that you can take your power back and change your life situation right now, today, if you want to. No matter what your present life situation is right now, today!

Changing our life situation – one thought at a time

But how do we do this? That's the big question. If we are only subject to what we hold in mind, how do we use the power of our minds wisely to change what we are holding in mind? To change our focus and thus our experience? Once again, awareness is the key. Awareness is the only way. Awareness is the prerequisite for any kind of personal change. You can't change anything if you're not aware of what's going on. You can't change anything if you are not aware of what you are doing. But once you begin to notice, once you begin to become aware of what's going on in your head – and notice what you are focusing your attention on, then you can take your power back and do something about it. Little by little. And this is what awakening to the power of mind is all about. It's all about waking up to what's going on inside your head! Noticing what you're holding in mind. Noticing what you are focusing on. Now and now and now.

And remember: Nobody else can do it for you – nobody else can take it from you! Because you are the only thinker in your mind!

What you focus your attention on grows

So now that we know that we are only subject to what we hold in mind, let's go a little deeper into the ramifications of this understanding and look at another aspect of the power of our minds which says – *Not only are you subject to what you hold in mind, but the more you focus on something, the more you get of it!* This is another important aspect of this impersonal, universal mechanism which we all can observe and which is important for you to confirm for yourself. So that you can understand once and for all that whether you like it or not, this is the way the Universe works. You don't get a say in this matter; this is the way things are set up. Which means you can't change these universal mechanisms because they are just the way things are.

But understanding these mechanisms is also the key to freedom as I keep saying, over and over again. Because once you understand these mechanisms and can confirm them for yourself, you can better understand why you attract certain experiences into your life and you can also learn to better control what you experience and what you attract more of. Thus you can learn to navigate more wisely in your own life and live more happily and consciously using this understanding to master and better control your experience. (For more about these mental mechanisms or universal principles, see my book *The Mental Laws* or read about the Mental Laws in Part 1 of my book *The Awakening Human Being – A Guide to the Power of Mind*.)

Problem oriented or solution oriented?

One way of noticing the focus of your attention and what you are doing mentally is to ask yourself during the course of your day – in this present situation – am I problem-oriented or solution-oriented? Now what do I mean by this?

We can say that every situation is just what it is. That's the reality. The situation is just what's going on. What's happening in front of you. That is what is. But the big question is – how are you relating to this situation, this reality? What are you focusing your attention on in this present situation? Are you problem-oriented or solution-oriented? In other words, are you focusing on everything that's wrong with this situation and all the problems involved – or are you focusing on everything that's good about the situation and all the potential involved? This is important to notice because it is this choice – your focus – i.e. the way in which you are relating to and holding this event or situation – that determines your experience of the present moment as well as what you are attracting more of. Because what you focus your attention on grows in your experience.

It plays out like this. If you are focusing on everything that can go wrong with a situation or person, it will probably happen. And if you are focusing on all the potential and on everything good that could happen and all that you can learn from the situation, this too will probably happen. This is why we say Life is a self-fulfilling prophecy. We get what we believe we're going to get. Especially what we believe with conviction.

Let's take a concrete example of what I mean by our choice of focus. Let's look at parents and how, for example, they focus on their children. A parent can choose to focus on everything that's so-called "wrong" about a child. In other words, focus on what the kid is doing wrong, how the kid needs to improve, how clumsy the kid is, how unhelpful, rebellious, stupid, silly the child is. Or the very same parent can choose to focus on all the strengths and talents this child has – and praise the child and encourage the child to build on whatever strengths and talents the child actually does have. And let's be completely clear about this – in both cases, we are talking about the exact same child. We are talking about a child who is good at some things and not so good at other things. (This is the reality about all children.) The child who sometimes does stuff the parents don't approve of and the child who is at times goofy and the child who is also precious and sweet. It's all the same child. But the choice of the parent's focus can make all the difference in the world as to how the parents experience life with this child and how this child grows and develops and perceives himself or herself and the world. That is why the Wise know the power of praise and blessing, especially when it comes to children. (For more about this mechanism see "The Power of Praise and Blessing" in my book *The Road to Power – Fast Food for the Soul*.)

Using the power of focus to support healing and self-empowerment

So now that we understand this mechanism – the power of our focus – how can we use this understanding to support ourselves (and other people) during the healing and recovery processes we have been discussing in this book? How can we use the power of our minds wisely in connection with processes and exercises like Truth Telling and Emotional Decompression – described in this section of the book? There are many, many ways we can do this, so I will try to outline a few for you.

In general, we can use the power of our minds and the power of focus to strengthen The Functional Adult in us. Please see Healing Process No. 1: *The Functional Adult and the Wounded Inner Child* to remind yourself of this dynamic. Focusing on the strengths of our Functional Adult during the healing and recovery process can be a very powerful and wise thing to do especially when we are using the various techniques like Truth Telling and Emotional Decompression. In other words, focusing on our strengths is a good way to prepare ourselves when we are accessing our past experiences and getting in touch with the old energy, which I call The Wounded Inner Child. So when we go back into the so-called "darkness" or emotional pain of some of our previous life experiences and start releasing this old energy (which can be stressful and unpleasant), it is a good idea to build up and fortify oneself by spending some time focusing on the strengths and resources we have today as Functional

Adults (i.e. the grown-up people we are now). When we do this, we will feel safer and more secure and more able to deal with the pain, sorrow and anger expressed by the Wounded Inner Child when it comes up to be released.

Here are some techniques you can use to strengthen the Functional Adult in yourself or in others.

Make a Gratitude List

A good place to start is by noticing how good your life already is in general. You can do this by making gratitude lists. To make a gratitude list, take out a piece of paper and write on the top of the page "I am grateful for" and then just start writing. Start with the simple (yet amazing) basic stuff in your life and write down things like:

- I am alive
- I can walk
- I can see
- I can hear
- I can talk
- I have food in my refrigerator
- I have a nice place to sleep
- My bed is so comfortable
- I have a good apartment
- I have a beautiful view from my window with trees outside
- There is heat in my apartment
- I have running water in the bathroom and a nice shower
- I have a job to go to
- I have money in the bank
- I have clothes to wear
- I have even more clothes in my closet
- I have several pairs of shoes to choose between
- I live in a country where there is peace and prosperity

- I have a computer and a cell phone and a TV
- I have some good friends
- I have people I can talk to
- The sun is shining today
- It's spring and the birds are chirping outside
- The flowers are lovely
- There is a beautiful tree over there
- My dog is wagging his tail
- I have wonderful children to play with
- I have a best friend
- She/he is so supportive
- I can call her when I need to talk and she listens
- I have other friends too
- I have wonderful books to read
- and... just keep going

Once you get started, you will discover that the list just goes on and on. Keep writing until you get a feeling of "uplift"-ment or until you feel your energy rising. If you do this on a regular basis, I guarantee the "tone" of your day and your life will change so that even if you do have some challenges at the moment, you will also be able to see and "feel" how much you actually do have in your life that is going well and how much support there is for you. And this is especially important to remind ourselves of when we go back and explore painful past situations and experiences. This is an excellent way to prepare and stabilize yourself – and stand in your power.

Another good way of making a gratitude list is to focus on all the people in your life who you love and all the people who love you. Make a list of friends, family and colleagues who are important in your life. Spend some time thinking about them and appreciating them. Think about how much they help you (think of specific situations) or how good it is to be able to talk to some of these people or just to know that they are there.

Remember – what you focus your attention on grows in your experience!

Make a Strength List

Another good way to strengthen the Functional Adult in you is to remind yourself of all your strengths. Take out a piece of paper and write your name at the top. Then start writing down all the good qualities about yourself that you can think of. (And don't be shy here. You don't have to show this list to anyone. This is for you. For your eyes only.) For example, you might write…

I am:

- intelligent
- well educated
- a good talker
- well read
- sociable
- I like people
- friendly
- empathic
- kind
- creative
- a good cook
- fit
- a good dancer
- good at fixing things
- generous
- a good sense of humor
- good organizer
- like to work
- like to help other people
- etc.

Keep going until you can't think of any more qualities that characterize you. And then look at your list every day. If you are brave, you can hang it on your refrigerator or somewhere where you will notice it. And read it every day. If you are shy about doing this exercise (why are you shy?) put your list somewhere where other people cannot see it. But remember to take your list out each day and look at it. And when you look at your list, remind yourself that this is not some abstract exercise about some make-believe person out there – this is YOU we are talking about. So notice your strengths and keep reminding yourself of who you really are and of all you've got going for yourself. And when you think of more qualities, well just add them to your list. (For more about making a Strength List, see Healing Process No. 1: *The Functional Adult and the Wounded Inner Child*.)

Make an Achievements List

Another good way to become more aware of your strengths is to write down some of the things you are proud of having achieved in your life. For example:

1) I started my own business
2) I am brave enough to go to therapy and work on my issues
3) I am going to school and getting an education
4) I ran a marathon
5) I had the courage and clarity to end my unfulfilling marriage
6) I dare being single again
7) I walked the Camino
8) I went on a long trip by myself
9) I had the courage to speak up at work
10) I said "no" even though I was under a lot of pressure to say "yes"
11) I am trying to "walk my talk"

Then for each thing that you are proud of having achieved, you can ask yourself: What strengths or qualities enabled me to achieve this? If, for example, you started your own business, what strengths or qualities enabled you to do this? Was it courage? Determination? Intelligence? Discipline? Vision? Creativity? Patience? Hard work? Good people skills? Write down whatever comes to mind (and be honest with yourself). You might be surprised to find that you have strengths and qualities you never really noticed before.

Make a Resource List

You can follow this by making a Resource List. By resources I mean people/things in the world around you that encourage and support you such as:

- my therapist or coach
- my wise grandmother
- my best friend who's always there for me
- going out in nature (always makes me relax)
- my teachers
- reading self-help books or spiritual books
- uplifting music
- going to massage or other body therapies
- the group meetings or 12-Step meetings I attend
- etc.

Again, when you focus on all the things and people around you who actually support and contribute to your well-being and safety and good life, it really does feel good. Plus we may begin to notice and be aware of people and circumstances that we may have taken for granted. And just waking up to this and focusing our attention on this, always brings more of a sense of gratitude into our lives along with an increased sense of ease and safety. Once again, we all have so much to be grateful for that we are just taking for granted. Noticing the Good in our lives makes the Good grow! That is the law.

The Power Questions

Anthony Robbins' Power Questions are another good tool you can use to remind yourself of all the good in your life and help you strengthen yourself. Ask yourself these questions every day for a while and notice how good it makes you feel.

Find at least three answers for each of these questions:

"1) What am I really excited about in my life?
2) What am I proud of in my life?
3) What am I grateful for?
4) Who loves me and who do I love?
5) What's great about my present situation?
6) What can I do today to make my life better?"

What can I give?

Another powerful way to strengthen the Functional Adult in you and to keep your energy high is to ask yourself what you can give or bring to any situation or relationship. Whether it be at work or with your partner or family and friends. Then make a list of the qualities that you can and do bring to the situation or relationship.

I can and do bring:

- good energy
- clarity
- dedication
- honesty
- loyalty
- sincerity
- presence

- integrity
- dedication
- strength
- reliability
- practical skills
- willingness
- common sense
- understanding
- generosity
- vision
- expertise in…
- vision
- imagination
- empathy
- compassion
- kindness
- good communication skills

And so on… And don't be shy. Think of and recognize all the good you are capable of bringing to any situation. Acknowledge that you are a capable and powerful human being and that there is no limit to the Good you can contribute to any and every situation and relationship you find yourself in. This is what healthy self-care and self-empowerment are all about. Acknowledge who you are and walk tall.

Use these exercises regularly

All the exercises suggested here are ways in which you can use the power of your mind to focus on all the Good you already have in your life and strengthen yourself, regardless of the challenges you may be facing at the present moment. But again, for these exercises to work, you have to do them more than once. To obtain maximum benefit, these simple exercises should become a part of your regular practice – focal points you can use in your daily life to navigate wisely on your journey of recovery towards more and more peace of mind and self-empowerment. Other good focal points to contemplate and meditate on regularly are, of course, the Healthy Models described in this book such as Healthy Model No. 6: *You Have Inherent Worth* or Healthy Model No. 7: *You Have an Inner Compass.*

And remember, it is especially important to remember and do these exercises when you are feeling challenged, stressed, anxious or depressed – or when your wounded inner child is triggered and unhappy. Then it can be especially helpful to balance whatever emotional pain you may be going through by focusing on your many strengths and resources.

Because remember the Universal Law of mind: **Whatever you focus your attention on grows in your experience!**

Reprogramming yourself

And finally, no matter what you're doing or how you feel, I highly recommend you use the world-famous mantra to reprogram yourself:

"EVERY DAY IN EVERY WAY,
I AM GETTING BETTER AND BETTER"

This powerful mantra was created by the French physician Émile Coué (1857-1926) to help people reprogram themselves and heal themselves of all kinds of illnesses and psychological problems. Coué, who was a medical doctor in France and a pioneer in the power of the mind, successfully treated thousands of patients with this mantra. All you have to do is repeat this mantra aloud – with feeling – 15 times in a row, three times a day, each and every day. It's good to do it first thing in the morning, then in the middle of the day, and then at night right before you go to bed. Keep on reprogramming yourself with this powerful thought – and then expect wonderful things to happen!

It takes time and it takes practice

Once we begin to understand the mechanism and the power of our minds in determining our experiences, we also usually discover that it's not always easy to put this new understanding into practice. So even though we really try to be mindful of what we are holding in mind and even though we do the various exercises and really want to change our focus and our thinking patterns, most of us discover it can be really difficult to change the thought stream. Now why is this so? Why is it so difficult to change the thought stream?

It's difficult because even though we understand the mechanism, we all have very strong mental habits. Every one of us does. And this is because we have all been practicing our own personal mental habits for a very long time (since early childhood). Because we have all been programmed from an early age into thinking and believing in very specific ways, and as a result, these belief systems and patterns of thinking have become the usual way that we focus on and regard things. As I said before, we have been doing this quite unconsciously for most of our lives. It's just the way it is. It's just the way we were brought up. It's what we learned from our parents and teachers and family and society in general, so these mental habits have gained a lot of momentum. Which means it's not so easy to just switch to new ways of thinking, and to think more positively and constructively. Especially if you have been trained to think negatively. This is what many of us discover when we start to understand that our focus determines our experience and that what we focus our attention on grows.

But again, even if this may be difficult, especially in the start, it is possible to learn to change your focus and thus change your experiences. But it does take time and it does take practice. Regular daily practice. So when you set out to understand and apply these principles and decide to change the way you think and live, it's really important to understand and remind yourself over and over again that changing the direction of your thought stream and your life experience is no easy task. It's not something that just happens because you want it to happen. It's not enough to just read about all this in books (like this one), you actually have to work at it. You actually have to do it day after day. You actually have to be conscious of what's going on in your mind and then consciously choose to change the direction of your thoughts. For example, by doing the exercises suggested above. So yes, it takes work. Real, conscious work. Real mindfulness. Which is why I call this process "Mental Training"!

Mental Training

So keep reminding yourself that "Mental Training" takes time and it takes effort. Mental Training – learning to consciously change the direction of your thought – is just like learning any other new skill. If, for example, you want to learn to play the piano, you know it's not enough to buy a piano and put it in your living room. You can't just sit there and look at the piano and then get up and play it. You have to actually take piano lessons, and then sit down and practice playing the piano, every day. And you have to practice a lot, not just for a couple of days. But if you do this, if you do practice, then eventually, you'll be able to play some tunes. And it's the same with learning to change your focus and think in new, more positive, life-giving ways. It takes practice. Real practice and dedication. And it takes time. But the results are so amazing that it's well worth the time and effort it takes to learn to make this important shift in your focus. Because your whole life will change.

For more about how to shift your focus and train yourself to think more positively and raise your energy, see my books *The Road to Power – Fast Food for the Soul* Books 1 & 2 and *The Awakening Human Being – A Guide to the Power of Mind*. These books are only about the power of focus, and how to become the master of your focus and thus create the life you want to live. The books are filled with concrete exercises that can help you train your mind into new positive ways of thinking and feeling – and thus change your life experience.

Healing Process No. 8

The Great Universal Intelligence – the Greatest Healing Power of All

When we are doing inner work, especially deep inner work, like going to therapy, releasing old pain or trauma, going into the difficulties and darkness of our lives to heal ourselves, it is important to balance all of this by focusing on all our strengths and resources and on all the Good in our lives as explained in the previous chapter, Healing Process No. 7, about how to use the power of the mind wisely. In addition to using the power of our minds to focus on the positive aspects of our lives, we can use the power of our minds to focus on the greatest comfort and support of all, which is the Great Universal Intelligence which created all of this Life, including us.

Now what exactly do I mean by this and how do we do it?

I suggest we start by noticing who or what is making all of this Life happen.

Starting simple

Let's start by taking a look at the reality of this world that surrounds us. Let's start with something simple and obvious like noticing that the sun came up this morning. Now that you remember that, yes, the sun did come up this morning, I can ask you – did you make this happen? Did you make the sun come up this morning? Was it something that you did or did the sun just come up, all by itself? I am pretty sure that you will answer that, yes the sun did come up this morning, but it did so without your help. Then I could also ask you – and what about the planets orbiting in space – are you making all that happen? And again you will most probably answer, it isn't you. And if I continue along this line and ask you – what about the trees

289

growing outside your window and the grass and all the plants? Are you making all that happen? And what about the seas and the oceans and all the fish and all the other animals? Are you making any of them happen? And again… most probably, you will answer that you are not making any of this happen.

But the reality is that all of this is happening. It is something we can all see and confirm for ourselves. We can all see that the sun does come up every morning and that the planets are revolving around the sun in perfect harmony every day and that the plants are arising and growing, and the animals are here, there and everywhere – and that all this is happening, and we are not making it happen. We are not doing it. Not you and not me. But it is happening anyway.

From this, we can conclude that there is some Greater Force or Greater Intelligence that is creating, manifesting and organizing this amazing Web of Life, this amazing dance, which is our Cosmos, that is unfolding all around us. There is some Greater Intelligence or Force which is creating and orchestrating all of this, which I will call for convenience – the Great Universal Intelligence. This Great Universal Intelligence, which is this greater creative Force or Power or Intelligence (or whatever else you might want to call it), that is organizing and orchestrating and coordinating the unfolding of Life all around us. Something is there and this something is doing all of this. It's obvious. You can see it unfolding wherever you look.

Look at you and your body

We can also ask the same questions and come to the same conclusions when we look at ourselves. So let's give that a try.

If you take a look at yourself, I can ask you – did you create your own body? Did you make yourself appear in this body? Again, the answer is the same. In all probability you will answer no! You did not make you happen, but again, here you are! You are here in this body, right here, right now. So again, something greater, some greater intelligence, which is far more intelligent than you or I, has organized and animated and manifested YOU! Pretty amazing to think about, isn't it?

The other thing about you (and me) is that now that we are here, we're still not "doing" us. By this I mean, you are not making yourself "be", you are just happening! Just think about it. Do you sit up all night and tell your heart to beat? No, you don't. Yet your heart beats all night long all by itself, without you telling it what to do, or watching it, or doing anything. It just does. Your heart just beats. The same goes for your lungs, which continue to breathe the air in and out, in and out. And the same with your digestion, which keeps on digesting your food, and all the other millions and trillions of cells and processes in your body, which are all going on all by themselves – without any thought, or direction, or interference from you or me. So again, there is some greater intelligence at work here. There is some greater Force or Intelligence that has manifested you and me and everyone else, and which is now animating and coordinating these amazing physical bodies, which we all have.

Just think about the intelligence of our bodies!

If, for example, you cut your finger with a knife while you are out in the kitchen preparing lunch and your finger starts to bleed... what do you do? Probably you will wash your finger off and then put a bandage on it. And once your finger is all bandaged up, you will probably just forget all about it. You'll just forget it and leave it alone. Then a couple of days later, you'll take off the bandage and see what you knew would happen – the cut has grown back together. All by itself, just like you knew it would. And it all happened by itself, so to speak. It all happened automatically. It just did.

You didn't sit there looking at your finger, all day long and all night long, telling the cells of your body to grow back together. The cells in your body knew what do to and they did it automatically – without any direction from you or interference from you. So who or what was doing it? Again, there is, obviously, some Greater Intelligence at work here. Obviously! Some Greater Intelligence or organizing power that has created and manifested all of creation including you and me!

Now since this Great Universal Intelligence created you and is animating you, it must also be *in you* and it must be manifesting itself in and *through you*! Pretty amazing when we think about it, which is why it is a good idea to spend some time contemplating this. Contemplating that there apparently is a Greater Universal Intelligence that created all of Life, including you. Contemplating what this probably means is a good idea... because then you will discover that not only must you be directly connected to this great Universal Force, you must also be an expression of, or individualization of, this Force... which also means that you must have all the qualities of it, which is definitely something worth noticing and thinking about.

Continue to contemplate

This is why it is so important to continue to contemplate the obvious reality that there is a Greater Universal Intelligence, an intelligence which is greater than yours or mine, which is clearly running the show. Because when you do this, it will give you greater and greater confidence in the fact that you are, and always have been, totally safe. Totally held in the arms of this Greater Intelligence. And that everything is actually being taken care of. Including everything about you. This will give you confidence that there is some greater mechanism, some greater intelligence, which is harmonizing and coordinating everything in Nature and in our world – whether it is inside our bodies or outside. And that this Power or Force is not only fully present within you, but also knows you and knows when and where and how to restore balance and harmony in you and your system, in other words, in your body and mind.

And the really cool thing about all this is that you will also know when this is happening, even if you oftentimes overlook this information. But the truth is you actually do know when balance and harmony are being re-established within you. And you know this because you have an Inner Compass which is always letting you know by means of your emotions whether you are moving in the direction of balance and harmony or not. Quite simply because when you move in the direction of balance and harmony, you just "feel" better. And this is what healing and recovery are all about. Moving, little by little, in the direction of balance and harmony, little by little in the direction of what feels better.

This means you can also know, if you pay attention, what the next logical or next best step for you in your healing and recovery process is. Your Inner Compass will let you know which exercises or which chapters in this book (or in any other book or books) are best suited for you, based on where you are right now. And you will know this because you can know what feels best. You can "feel", and therefore know, which exercise or exercises or which chapter or chapters you are most attracted to. You know what gives you more of a sense of ease and comfort... and yes, you can and do know this, if you pay attention to the signals coming from within you. And these signals are the Great Universal Intelligence working in and through you, always giving you the information you need for the next step on your healing journey.

The same holds true if you are a therapist. In addition to your training, you also have an Inner Compass that will help you know and "feel" your way to what is the next best step for each one of your clients. And you will know this by "feeling" where there is more of a sense of ease and flow, and more of a sense of comfort for your client. You will know what direction gives your client glimpses of relief and maybe even moments of joy. And interestingly enough, it's not always what your rational mind thinks the next best step is going to be; rather it is often a deeper knowing that comes from within. That comes from your Inner Compass which is your direct connection to the Great Universal Intelligence that is always working to re-establish balance and harmony in you and in everyone else. So whether you are someone working on your own healing process or are a therapist helping others – or both – this is what all the Healthy Models and Healing Processes in this book are designed to do. They are all designed to help you to find and re-establish – balance and harmony again. Each one of these Healthy Models and Healing Processes are designed to help you re-establish equilibrium in your life. But which one is the next best step for you? Only you can know that, only you can feel your way into the next best step which is the right means for you, depending on who you are and where you are on your journey. Depending on who you are and where you are on this never-ending journey which each one of us is traveling... traveling towards remembering and reconnecting with our own true Original Goodness.

Blessings to you on your way!

Recommended Reading

Books by Barbara Berger

The Power of the Mind

If you are looking for more information about the way the mind works and how the focus of our attention determines our experience, you will find this in the following books of mine:

The Road to Power – Fast Food for the Soul

The Road to Power 2 – More Fast Food for the Soul

The Awakening Human Being – A Guide to the Power of Mind (with Tim Ray)

The Mental Laws – Understanding the Way the Mind Works

Sane Self Talk – Cultivating the Voice of Sanity Within

The Spiritual Pathway – A Guide to the Joys of Awakening and Soul Evolution

Gateway to Grace – Barbara Berger's Guide to User-Friendly Meditation

Guidance

For more information about the significance of our emotions and the mechanism which I call the Inner Compass, see:

Find and Follow Your Inner Compass – Instant Guidance in an Age of Information Overload

Constructive Communication and Assertiveness Training

Are You Happy Now? 10 Ways to Live a Happy Life (Chapters 3 & 5)

Find and Follow Your Inner Compass – Instant Guidance in an Age of Information Overload (Part 2 of the book)

Sane Self Talk – Cultivating the Voice of Sanity Within

Mindfulness, Present Moment Awareness, Questioning our Thinking

For a more in-depth exploration of being mindful and living fully present in the moment – and how we can question our thinking and stop resisting what is, see my books:

Are You Happy Now? 10 Ways to Live a Happy Life

Sane Self Talk – Cultivating the Voice of Sanity Within

Books by other authors and teachers

There are a handful of other teachers and authors who explore some of the various issues and approaches discussed in this book. They include:

Melody Beattie
- *Codependent No More*
- *Beyond Codependency*

John Bradshaw
- *Homecoming – Reclaiming and Championing Your Inner Child*
- *Family Secrets*

Harriet B. Braiker
- *The Disease to Please*

Mary Baker Eddy
- *Science and Health with Key to the Scriptures*

Emmet Fox
- *Power Through Constructive Thinking*

Howard Halpern
- *How to Break Your Addiction to a Person*

David R. Hawkins
- *Healing and Recovery*
- *Transcending the Levels of Consciousness*
- *Truth vs. Falsehood*
- *Power vs. Force*
- *Letting Go*

Judith Lewis Herman
- *Trauma and Recovery*

The Teachings of Abraham – through Esther and Jerry Hicks
- *Ask and It Is Given*
- *The Vortex*

Byron Katie
- *Loving What Is*
- *I Need Your Love – Is That True?*

Peter A. Levine
- *Waking the Tiger – Healing Trauma*
- *Healing Trauma*

Pia Mellody
- *Facing Codependence*
- *Facing Love Addiction*
- *The Intimacy Factor*

Tim Ray
- *Starbrow*
- *Starwarrior*
- *101 Relationship Myths*

Manuel J. Smith
- *When I Say No, I Feel Guilty*

Eckhart Tolle
- *The Power of Now*
- *A New Earth*

Claire Weekes
- *Essential Help for Your Nerves*

Twelve-Step Programs and literature

The Declaration of Independence & The Constitution of the United States

O-BOOKS

SPIRITUALITY

O is a symbol of the world, of oneness and unity; this eye represents knowledge and insight. We publish titles on general spirituality and living a spiritual life. We aim to inform and help you on your own journey in this life.

If you have enjoyed this book, why not tell other readers by posting a review on your preferred book site?

Recent bestsellers from O-Books are:

Heart of Tantric Sex
Diana Richardson
Revealing Eastern secrets of deep love and intimacy to Western couples.
Paperback: 978-1-90381-637-0 ebook: 978-1-84694-637-0

Crystal Prescriptions
The A-Z guide to over 1,200 symptoms and their healing crystals
Judy Hall
The first in the popular series of eight books, this handy little guide is packed as tight as a pill-bottle with crystal remedies for ailments.
Paperback: 978-1-90504-740-6 ebook: 978-1-84694-629-5

Take Me To Truth
Undoing the Ego
Nouk Sanchez, Tomas Vieira
The best-selling step-by-step book on shedding the Ego, using the teachings of *A Course In Miracles*.
Paperback: 978-1-84694-050-7 ebook: 978-1-84694-654-7

The 7 Myths about Love...Actually!
The Journey from your HEAD to the HEART of your SOUL
Mike George
Smashes all the myths about LOVE.
Paperback: 978-1-84694-288-4 ebook: 978-1-84694-682-0

The Holy Spirit's Interpretation of the New Testament
A Course in Understanding and Acceptance
Regina Dawn Akers
Following on from the strength of *A Course In Miracles*, NTI teaches us how to experience the love and oneness of God.
Paperback: 978-1-84694-085-9 ebook: 978-1-78099-083-5

The Message of A Course In Miracles
A translation of the Text in plain language
Elizabeth A. Cronkhite
A translation of *A Course in Miracles* into plain, everyday language for anyone seeking inner peace. The companion volume, *Practicing A Course In Miracles*, offers practical lessons and mentoring.
Paperback: 978-1-84694-319-5 ebook: 978-1-84694-642-4

Your Simple Path
Find Happiness in every step
Ian Tucker
A guide to helping us reconnect with what is really important in our lives.
Paperback: 978-1-78279-349-6 ebook: 978-1-78279-348-9

365 Days of Wisdom
Daily Messages To Inspire You Through The Year
Dadi Janki
Daily messages which cool the mind, warm the heart and guide you along your journey.
Paperback: 978-1-84694-863-3 ebook: 978-1-84694-864-0

Body of Wisdom
Women's Spiritual Power and How it Serves
Hilary Hart
Bringing together the dreams and experiences of women across the world with today's most visionary spiritual teachers.
Paperback: 978-1-78099-696-7 ebook: 978-1-78099-695-0

Dying to Be Free
From Enforced Secrecy to Near Death to True Transformation
Hannah Robinson
After an unexpected accident and near-death experience, Hannah Robinson found herself radically transforming her life, while a remarkable new insight altered her relationship with her father, a practising Catholic priest.
Paperback: 978-1-78535-254-6 ebook: 978-1-78535-255-3

The Ecology of the Soul
A Manual of Peace, Power and Personal Growth for Real People
in the Real World
Aidan Walker
Balance your own inner Ecology of the Soul to regain your
natural state of peace, power and wellbeing.
Paperback: 978-1-78279-850-7 ebook: 978-1-78279-849-1

Not I, Not other than I
The Life and Teachings of Russel Williams
Steve Taylor, Russel Williams
The miraculous life and inspiring teachings of one of the World's
greatest living Sages.
Paperback: 978-1-78279-729-6 ebook: 978-1-78279-728-9

On the Other Side of Love
A woman's unconventional journey towards wisdom
Muriel Maufroy
When life has lost all meaning, what do you do?
Paperback: 978-1-78535-281-2 ebook: 978-1-78535-282-9

Practicing A Course In Miracles
A translation of the Workbook in plain language, with
mentor's notes
Elizabeth A. Cronkhite
The practical second and third volumes of The Plain-Language
A Course In Miracles.
Paperback: 978-1-84694-403-1 ebook: 978-1-78099-072-9

Quantum Bliss
The Quantum Mechanics of Happiness, Abundance, and Health
George S. Mentz
Quantum Bliss is the breakthrough summary of success and spirituality secrets that customers have been waiting for.
Paperback: 978-1-78535-203-4 ebook: 978-1-78535-204-1

The Upside Down Mountain
Mags MacKean
A must-read for anyone weary of chasing success and happiness – one woman's inspirational journey swapping the uphill slog for the downhill slope.
Paperback: 978-1-78535-171-6 ebook: 978-1-78535-172-3

Your Personal Tuning Fork
The Endocrine System
Deborah Bates
Discover your body's health secret, the endocrine system, and 'twang' your way to sustainable health!
Paperback: 978-1-84694-503-8 ebook: 978-1-78099-697-4

Readers of ebooks can buy or view any of these bestsellers by clicking on the live link in the title. Most titles are published in paperback and as an ebook. Paperbacks are available in traditional bookshops. Both print and ebook formats are available online.
Find more titles and sign up to our readers' newsletter at
http://www.johnhuntpublishing.com/mind-body-spirit
Follow us on Facebook at https://www.facebook.com/OBooks/
and Twitter at https://twitter.com/obooks